The Living and the Dead

TOBY AUSTIN LOCKE

The Living and the Dead

An Essay on the Tendential Continuities of Life and Death

Published by Repeater Books

An imprint of Watkins Media Ltd
19-21 Cecil Court
London
WC2N 4EZ
UK

www.repeaterbooks.com
A Repeater Books paperback original 2016
1

Distributed in the United States by Random House, Inc., New York.

ISBN: 978-1-910924-32-7
Ebook ISBN: 978-1-910924-33-4

Cover design: Johnny Bull
Typography and typesetting: Jan Middendorp
Typefaces: Chaparral Pro, Absara Sans, Alegreya Italic
Printed and bound in Great Britain

What heaven, what pleasure does your life offer which outweighs death's delights? Doesn't all that inspires us bear the color of the Night? It bears you mother-like, and you all your magnificence to her.

—Novalis

But if death calls, although the noise of the call fills the night, the call is a kind of profound silence. The response itself is stripped of every possible meaning. This is gripping: the greatest voluptuousness that the heart endures, a morose, crushing voluptuousness, a boundless heaviness.

—Georges Bataille

Contents

*A Preamble
by Way of
Impotent
Apology*

My impotence to expound the question of death must be made clear from the offset. To claim to be able to tell you what death is, how it functions, the manner in which it reveals itself to us, would be fundamentally dishonest. There can be no normative definition or understanding of death. But this does not make it a topic unworthy of discussion. Death stands before us as unknowable, but at the same time as inevitable. That life is run through with death and death with life is one of those rare safe things we can say. But this intertwining simultaneously reveals the most profound feeling as regards death; namely, that the very conditions of our becoming are entangled with and inextricably associated to unknowable conditions, conditions that our myopia, our short-sightedness and tunnel vision, forever leave floating before us just beyond the reach of clear perception.

It is death that installs nonknowledge at the base of knowledge and misosophy at the base of philosophy. As that of which all of the living are aware, and fleeing towards, and yet remains unknowable, death reminds us not only of our own finitude and mortality, but also of our impotence, myopia and powerlessness, our foolishness and ignorance. For this reason, among others, to speak of death is in one sense the greatest and cruellest act of tragicomedy for it brings into the space of knowledge and discourse that which is unknowable and which always exceeds knowledge. The theorist or philosopher confronting death confronts their own child-like foolishness, their own inability to think. And what is more, it denies the very foundations of transcendent metaphysics—that system of knowledge that for so long assured us of our own divinity, eternity and superiority.

Georges Bataille puts it as follows:

Death teaches nothing, since we lose the benefit of the instruction that it might offer us by dying. It's true, we think about the death of the other. We reconcile the impression that the death of the other gives us with ourselves. We often imagine ourselves in the position of those who we see dying, but we can only justifiably do this on the condition of living. Reflection on death is much more seriously derisive than living, it is always scattering our attention, and we speak in vain about exerting ourselves, when death is at stake.

Of course, talking about death is the most profound practical joke.[3]

Alongside this cautionary word against my own impotence in approaching the question of death I must also offer the following caution. Throughout the pages that follow I shall draw upon a range of writers, ideas and perspectives, but I will do so in a manner that makes no claim to be representing either a universal statement of what death may mean, or indeed what any of the authors and thinkers themselves may have meant. This is perhaps unnecessary to say, but it is nonetheless important to make it clear from the beginning; namely a rejection of the notion that in drawing forth an idea the entire system of thought and philosophy from which it is drawn must come with it. Such approaches, those that seek to uncover the consistency and actuality of a mode of thought, fail to confront the consideration above — namely that we are integrally myopic — but perhaps worse than that, they commit the cardinal sin of academia and are quite simply dull and uninteresting. In producing any kind of work, repetition is integral, but not to the extent that it is all that is offered. Indeed such faithful repetition is neither possible nor desirable; when it is sought we fail to approach that which is most vital and active in thought — the *terra incognita*, the unknown territory, not of philosophy, but of misosophy, that is a hatred of stratified systems of knowledge and received wisdom. I have little interest in paying homage to the proper nouns of monumental history or marching tirelessly through the received wisdom of the ages. To do so fails to appreciate what is perhaps the most enthralling and potent element of thought—namely its basis in misosophy.

In this spirit I would also like to make a brief comment on the use of ideas and texts both theoretical and ethnographic in the pages that follow. The displacement of concepts and words from their original context has been heavily criticised, and not without good reason. It is clear that ideas and practices invariably require vast contextualising frameworks and their removal from these frameworks can lead to dangerous distortions. However, with this said, rigid refusal to allow for interfaces between the conceptual systems of varying locations and times can also run into danger of producing the kind of attitude that Guattari referred to as "a kind of cultural polycentricism, a multiplication of ethnocentrism." [4] Through such rigid insistence that notions remain only within their original context we become caught in a situation where the world is comprised of isolated bubbles incapable of meaningful communication with one another—the reality of others becomes inaccessible and in some sense denied. For my own part, I seek to aim for, and undoubtedly do not achieve, a multiplication of truths through conversations and negotiations between a diversity of perspectives. In this way we return to the famous many eyes, and many truths, of even the sphinx[5]—not in a manner that makes those eyes and perspectives inaccessible, but rather in a manner that allows for a pluralisation of truth that becomes impossible to approach through the kind of conceptual isolation described above.

That Nietzsche refers to the sphinx, a mythical being, is significant for it begins the dismantlement of the notion that truth, reason and thought belong only to the human, and indeed the living. This is an attitude that, as far as anthropology is concerned, has been reignited recently in the works of authors like Eduardo Viveiros de Castro and Eduardo Kohn. It is an attitude that allows for the transformation that comes with attempts to leave one's point of view, and engages in the radical transformations that come about through changing one's position and thus the horizons towards which one can gaze and travel; and it is an attitude which in turn denies the dogmatism which comes with absolutely affirming one's immovable position. It is an attitude that allows for conversation and interaction between diverse and radically different points of view whilst not attempting to explain them through a theoretical meta-language or falling into the solipsistic isolation of traditional modes of relativism, it is an attitude which allows for difference to be articulated and enter into negotiation without it being flattened out or explained away.

As such, these pages and passages do not seek explication, but are offered up simply as exploratory probes—passages of thought that entertain a topic that is by its very nature unknowable and unknown. But it is this unknowableness that makes the topic so potent, just as we find paradox to be one of the highest marks of truth.[6] Indeed, this is a project that goes well beyond the current book, and I have no doubt that no matter how many words were written, its insufficiency, inconsistency and even incoherence would never be overcome; but nonetheless, not only due to this, death remains at the very foundation of thought in a manner parallel to misosophy's insistence within philosophy, and this is a parallel of great significance.

These words were written over a course of time that saw me pass through many births, deaths and lives. The compulsion to write these words came, at least from one trajectory, from experiencing the death of one who had been close to me. Along another but not disconnected trajectory, these words were written amidst a range of transformations, that is tiny births and deaths, in which relationships were fundamentally altered, that entity which we poorly attempt to name as the self dissolved, and the bonds between people underwent great ruptures. As such, acknowledgement cannot directly be made of the innumerable sources of inspiration and contribution to these words, but those with whom my lives and deaths have been entangled each in different ways have formed part of the words that are now written here.

On an intellectual and literary level, it is important to acknowledge two foundations to the following pages. One we have already mentioned as Georges Bataille, and the other, perhaps less directly, is Novalis. As such, two of the spurring influences on this work are romanticism and surrealism. The need for both these modes not only of thought, but also of experience and feeling, is great at the present time. What the confusing, irrational and uncanny space of surrealism, and the hopeful, joyful and tragic domain of romanticism offer us are profound antidotes to the suppressive forces of rationalisation and functionalisation that seem to dominate so many domains today and that leave us in a disenchanted world of capital and a particular kind of prominent false-scientificity devoid of affirmation and determination. In short, romanticism and surrealism combined grant us the potential to reclaim our sovereignty, to re-enchant our becoming, and to stand in the *untimely*.

Introduction

Life forever holds within itself, coiled at the very centre of its unfolding, the fearful promise of death. That death, emerging from the shadows of the living, from the darkness that forever follows the living, brings about an absolute end-of-life, brings down its sickle upon the vitality of the existent in order to return it to nonexistence. Death, then—the absolute, final end-of-life—is that nothingness, that emptiness, that hollow darkness, which is forever stalking the living, anticipating that twilight upon which it may exercise its right to return ashes to ashes and dust to dust, restoring that which is living to the barren desolation of the non-living. This is the conception of death that has so often paralyzed thought, leaving us unable to fully appreciate the complexities and nuances of the relationship between the living and the dead.

Such a conception of death, as that which brings an absolute end-of-life, has been persistent, and for all good sense, and indeed philosophy, it appears as though it could be no other way. How can it be possible for one to speak of death other than as an absolute end-of-life? Is it not precisely a complete and absolute lack of life that is characteristic of death? It would appear foolish to attempt to think otherwise, to think death as something other than the final, absolute and total end-of-life. Nevertheless, in spite of its apparent stupidity, its total lack of good sense, its absurdity and indeed, as some might say, its impossibility, that is precisely the task to now be placed at hand: that of thinking life and death tendentially. That is to say, what is here sought is an exploration of the relationships between the continuous tendencies of the living and the nonliving. Our failure to think death in a manner other than what shall be referred to as the *finalist* conception does us great disservice.

This conception of death, as we have said, is pervasive, and with good reason; for to all good sense death can be nothing other than an end-of-life, an absolute and final end. As is customary within discussions of those means, systems and frameworks of knowledge known as *episteme* and indeed of the *episteme* itself — for we cannot pretend that we are an exception and that we may discourse beyond its limits — we may start by reading from Aristotle. In the *Nicomachean Ethics*, where the task is the question of an art of living, Aristotle confronts the question of death. He writes, "[n]ow the most terrible thing of all is death; for it is the end, and when a man is dead, nothing, we think, either good or evil can befall him any more."[7] Here, the *finalist* conception of death is stated clearly and precisely. The occurrence of death is that of rupture, it is that which brings an end-of-life and an end of affection, "for it is the end." Nothing may be brought into connection or relation with the dead. The living, in death, escape from their pharmacological entrapment by the ever-fluctuating duality of good–evil. Death is terrible. The dead may not be befallen by anything for they have already fallen to death and there is nowhere further to fall. Persistence, presence and duration are severed. The bottom has been reached.

But we must not simplify. Let us read on, for what Aristotle is considering here, in the foreground at least, is the role of Courage in living well. He continues,

> But even death, we should hold, does not in all circumstances give an opportunity for Courage: for instance we do not call a man courageous for facing death by drowning or disease. What form of death then is a test of Courage? Presumably that which is the noblest. Now the noblest form of death is death in battle, for it is encountered in the midst of the greatest and most noble of dangers. And this conclusion is borne out by the principle on which public honours are bestowed in republics and under monarchies. The courageous man, therefore, in the proper sense of the term, will be he who fearlessly confronts a noble death, or

some sudden peril that threatens death; and the perils of war answer this description most fully.[8]

Aristotle's questioning concerns the transition of life to death; that is, a transference between states that are clearly segmented, static and oppositional. The question of the Courage of death concerns the manner by which one transfers from living to dead, the door through which one passes in order to traverse the threshold between life and death. Death has already been established as being beyond affection, being beyond the ethical pharmacology of good–evil, poison–medicine, for death "is the end." It is the door through which one passes that is subject to the determinations of an ethics; the question of how to live in the face of the absolute end-of-life that is death.

The conclusion reached by Aristotle—that the Courageous and therefore good death is death in battle, death in the face of conflict—is reached by the consideration of "the principle on which public honours are bestowed in republics and under monarchies." The judgement of Courage, the determination of the good death, is determined by the living for "neither good nor evil can befall" the dead. It is only for the living that one dies Courageously. The threshold that stands between the living and the dead is subject to the determination of an ethics, but only from the side of the living, for the dead have already fallen and can fall no further. The states are total. The means of dying, the transference, only exists as the barrier between two states, and further only exists from the side of the living, for in death there is nothing, only a complete negation that would forbid any ethical determination. For the dead, then, there is nothing noble or Courageous about falling in battle. Courage only belongs to the living, to the living-in-the-face-of-death or the living-considering-the-death-of-others, the former being the state of those set to die in battle, the latter being the state of those bestowing "public honours."

The question of death then is set as an opposition between two states, one pertaining to ethics as the art of living, one pertaining to nothing. If death is a concern, if it becomes a question at all, it is only insofar as it concerns the living. The process of death, that is of dying, is not given the same treatment as the process of life, that is of living, the latter being the concern of ethics. The movement from life to death is lost. There is either life, for which there is a good death, or death, for which there is nothing. It is perhaps peculiar that Aristotle should reason in such a way, in a way that is both devoid of tendency and devoid of duration. Peculiar because this is the same Aristotle who will, in *Physics*, refute Zeno's paradox of motionless movement precisely by, in his own way, demonstrating the necessity of duration and connectivity.[9] But the arrow of Zeno persists in Aristotle's conception of death, it is the same succession of states, devoid of continuity and fluidity, that is at work in death becoming the absolute end-of-life, the state which ends the preceding state being entirely unconnected and unhampered by any tendential movement, any gradation. It is this lack of continuity and stubborn refusal of fluidity that is the basis of Zeno's staggering arrow, which will haunt *episteme* in the finalist conception of death. The life of one state ends absolutely and that which follows is absolutely different—there is no connection. But of course, we must not forget that as all good sense will tell us, death is an exception for it is the absolute end-of-life. It is that nothingness which stubbornly encroaches on the living, that negation which remains forever at the core of life. How else could it be?

Let us turn our attention back further. When Socrates states in *Phaedrus*[10] that writing has the capacity to destroy memory, what is at stake is not only the pharmacological character of technics,[11] its dual role as poison and medicine, but also death. It is a tendency of life towards the nonliving that is the basis of technicity, of the letter and tool, those nonliving organs of memory and action. Socrates opposes the destructive capacity of the dead letter, to the generative power of living words; for Socrates there is "another kind of speech, or word, which shows itself to be the legitimate brother of this bastard one."[12] Such a word is the word of the living, the word imbued with vitality, or as Phaedrus responds, "the living and breathing word of him who knows."[13] Life brings life, but death brings only death. The living word is legitimate in uncovering *logos*, the ground of reason or ordering principle of knowledge. And as such, this living word is that which may bring forth *logos* through discoursing, it is that word which may grasp its vitality in order to defend itself, may thrust itself, living as it is, towards truth and in turn uphold and defend this truth. Such a living word may respond, for in its utterance it is unified with living memory. The dead word of the inscribed letter threatens the vitality of memory, threatens it with destruction, threatens to condemn *logos* to remain hidden, to fall with the dead into the bleak domain of the nonliving. There is nothing for the dead letter precisely because it is dead.

To bring forth *logos*, to allow its emergence, we can only turn to active memory of the living word, unified as it is with truth, life and thought, determined as it is by the art of living, by the determinations of good–evil. The purity of the living word, its unity with intelligence, with the untainted idea must be guarded against its "bastard brother," that illegitimate, deformed sibling that would threaten its destruction. The unity of thought and word, of *logos* and discourse, is threatened by the artificial externality of the inscribed letter, by the disunity, disequilibrium and destruction that it will bring about, by the threat of death as an end of memory, as an end of the living memory of pure word brought about through the degradation of the dead memory of inscription. The dead inscribed word cannot adapt, defend or consider as does the live memory of speech.

Socrates fears the dead letter, but it appears he does not fear death. The *finalist* conception of death, for him, emerges not in the fear of his death, but it haunts him in the manner in which he approaches the inscribed letter. Socrates does not fear the unknown, but he does fear the destruction of the known. He fears the death of the known, the concealment of living *logos* by the dead tainted letter. But of his own death, it seems he cares little; "the state of death is one of two things: either it is virtually nothingness, so that the dead has no consciousness of anything, or it is, as people say, a change and migration of the soul from this to another place." [14] Socrates fears the realm of the nonliving in the form of the inscribed letter, but the death of his individuality scares him not. How is it that these two perspectives on death and the nonliving operate at once? How can it be that death is either nothing in the sense of an eternal-life of the soul, or nothing in the sense of a return to *nihil*, the hollow domain of nothingness? And how is it that death here constitutes itself in relation to life and life in relation to death?

In the pages that follow we will seek to establish that death is not the limit of life, it is not that which brings an end to living and it cannot be fairly represented by the sweeping of a scythe, by a movement of severing; neither can it be reduced to *nihil* in the sense of hollow nothingness, or nothing in relation to an eternal-life. We cannot see in death an end-of-life, and an after-of-life, but this does not mean we only have recourse to an afterlife; and so too, in life we do not see a lack of death, a total vitality that would remove us from the nonliving. In short, death is not the outside of life as life is not the outside of death. Many histories of thought have suffered greatly by a general failure to contemplate the continual game of life and death, the continual flux between the living and nonliving and the confusion and perspectival transformation such contemplation entails. In this sense then, these pages concern tendency and flux, the inseparability of two movements and passages of becoming that have often been placed in opposition to one another, and that have appeared as the limit of one another, as the severing of life and the escape from death. It is the premise of these pages that such a separation is not useful and does not fairly represent the complexity and interdependency of life and death that is vitality itself.

This use of language may appear peculiar; one may be tempted to respond that there's nothing death could possibly mean other than a lack of life, an end-of-life, that it is an absolute finality, that vitality only concerns the living. But this is precisely our task, to explore how death is constituted in life and life in death. The non-living and living speak with one another, dance with one another, and the echoes of their communication never cease to reverberate throughout one another. The nonliving live with the living, dwell with the living and inhabit the living, just as the living die with the dead, dwell with the dead and inhabit the dead. Their separation has been that of finality, of our inability to think beyond finality, in that beyond that would always be beyond precisely because it is beyond and thus cannot be brought forth from the beyond.

So how do we begin to think life and death beyond finality? How do we seek to grasp this beyond that continually remains beyond? How do we seek to approach that which is forever receding in the form of the horizon? Not in a beyond of life, or a beyond of death, but a beyond in so far as temporality always exceeds any moment, always exceeds any event, always demands a place and voice simultaneously in pasts, presents and futures. Not in a beyond that would be eschatological or teleological, that would reach a final goal or arrive at a final conclusion; but a beyond that would be tendential, that would be beyond in as far as it is of continual exchange and movement, a continual and powerful communication. How do we begin to think a beyond that is always so, a beyond that cannot be encapsulated in a presentation of a concept, but remains beyond precisely due to its inability to become static, precisely in its continual partiality, its eternal fluctuation?

This is what is at stake in these pages—the question of life and death without finality or originality, without ends or origins. It is a question through which we may try to reignite vitality, through which both the living and nonliving may be allowed to exist as continually fluctuating, incomplete tendencies and escape from the tyranny of state-hood and staticity, that tyranny that freezes the fluidity of becoming. It is a question through which we may live and die. It is a question through which we may reclaim life and death from their finalist conceptualisation and enact them in their infinitude as the unlimited grounds of possibility, in their entanglement in infinite series of latent and active potentialities.

But we must be clear that we do not seek salvation — that is, the continued existence of life after death, the immortality of the soul, the ability to find a universal meaning for the living. Rather we seek to approach a greater recognition of the relationship between living things and dead things for the benefit of both. To reduce the question of life and death to the question of the eternity of life and its salvation is to ignore the question of death, it is to turn away from its horizon and yet to continue to move towards it blindly, it is to reduce death to *nihil*, to an object of fear so great that it is not even looked upon; and such a homogenisation of death, its reduction to *nihil*, brings too a homogenisation of life which leaves us unable to appreciate the endless tiny deaths that confront us and through which we pass every day.

In this way the question of death is in some respects a question of scale, of the variances and nuances between the molecular and the molar, of becoming attuned to the great multiplicity of lives and deaths that exist beyond the grand notions of Life and Death. Just as when we move up and down scales when regarding matter and that which appeared to be one coherent object crumbles into a collation of multiplicity, so too when we move across the scales of life and death does the coherence of these concepts shatter. We bring into view innumerable tiny deaths and births. When we no longer only take the life and death of an organism as that which defines the concept of living and dying, all number of tiny deaths emerge: our exteriorization into technology, our sustenance, our formation, our endless relations to that which is not living. Just as a rock or plant when examined under a microscope shifts from being a bound, delimited object to becoming a porous and fluctuating space of exchange, movement and transition, so too does the barrier between the living and the dead.

So it is in a somewhat different sense that we can agree on the inevitability of death. No longer is it simply the absolute final end-of-life, but on the contrary its inevitability is located in the fact that it is necessary for life, it everywhere supports and extends life. Not simply because that which is living must be defined in relation to that which is not living, but because that which is living grows on a ground which is dead, feeds on sources that are dead, and is enriched by that which is dead. In this way death remains a no-matter-what in relation to life, an inevitability, as well as being seen from the no-matter-what[15] in a way that blurs and displaces its position as rupture; that is, as being a flat ontological plane in front of which death and life, that which is alive and that which is nonliving, are utterly equal and undifferentiated.

And so now our question becomes — how do we confront and stand before death without the promise of salvation? What happens when we make of death an object of affirmation and joy, rather than one of fear, sorrow and negation? What happens when we dance with death, as the absolute possibility of our being? What happens when we think of death through, beyond and against Heidegger, no longer as my ownmost possibility of being,[16] but as our affirmation of connectivity, with a They that is not a pejorative, but the formation of the us and so to the I? How do we stand forth into the beyond that death presents us with without a divine guide? What would a *Hymn to the Night*[17] sound like in the wake of the death of God?

CHAPTER 1

An Inside of Life

What Is Death? — What Is Life?

The question "What is death?" — asked as though it could be answered — demands of us the inverse question "What is life?" and to both of these questions we appear unable to formulate coherent logical responses. The question of life, and so too death, comes to stand for so much and at the same time so little, that the mind reels at the possibility of attempting an answer. It is true that for a long time now biology has been able to explain life in its own terms, but even here, as one approaches the borderlands, the edges of the black-boxed working definitions that scientists so often have to deploy, we find ambiguity, we find those entities that rest at the edges of life — the virus for instance. At what point do we come to say that something is living? And at what point do we deem it to be dead or nonliving? There are the explanations of the most reductive biological type that can provide a taxonomy of the living, but even these fall apart when confronted with the entities which rest at the margins of life, and even at the margins which separate one form of life from another. There are the broadest definitions of the most optimistic panvitalism and hylozoism, which make of life the only object of affirmation and joy, and find within all a powerful vital current permeating existence.

But our initial question was "What is death?" and already we have turned to the vitalistic point of view. The question of death carries with it the same problems, the same impossibilities of taxonomies, and the same blurring of boundaries upon approaching the borderlands. When we speak of the dead, to whom do we refer? When we speak of that which is nonliving, to what do we refer? Do, by death, we mean the passage of a living entity into a domain in which it is no longer living? For by that we can poorly understand the degradation of an individual organism,

25

but we do not grasp death and the dead, we do not even begin to grasp the heterogeneity of the nonliving. What would lie beyond the process of dying? This beyond of life has been a question for numerous religions and philosophies, and yet it remains a beyond that we cannot articulate precisely because it is a beyond to the domain of life that we declare to inhabit. What belongs to this domain of nonliving, dead entities that so haunts life?

The questions, those of the living and the dead, appear to present to us a matter of continuity and discontinuity that the so-called "Western" epistemes and their metaphysics of substance have trouble approaching. With minds shaped and geared towards tackling questions of static and solid entities, of objects, things and states, we seem unable to approach questions that concern a more basic, perhaps even primordial or abiogenetic, question of a tendential connectivity between two domains that we seem to insist upon positing as separate and contained: that of the active and vital living, and that of the passive and listless dead. The continuous nature of the living and the dead, their tendential relationship—that is, the positing of tendencies that lean towards life and tendencies that lean towards death but never entirely resolve themselves into two discontinuous and separate domains—appears to paralyse us. So convinced are we that the domain of the dead is set apart from the domain of the living that even the question of abiogenesis demands an origin of a schism between the space of life and the space of death.

We insist upon a separation between the world of life and the world of death, but in our horror at the consequences of this separation we come to exclude and diminish the importance of the dead domain: we condemn it to a shadowy spiritual world; we suppress it under the banner of universal or eternal life; we insist that the nonliving entities which we always already are together with are naught but tools and extensions of the living; we lock the dying away, hidden behind medicalised screens and pathological determinations; the environment becomes a backdrop upon which the important drama of life is enacted; the dead space of technology becomes but an extension of the living mind; the water cycle and patterns of rock formation become little more than entirely determined and mechanical processes; the accumulation of labour in the forms of capital are claimed to be no more than servants to their living masters. The domain of dead things, the domain of those things which we determine to not permit entry to the domain of life, becomes a secondary entity, and one that is separated from life.

So we return to our question — "What is death?" — and its inverse — "What is life?" — and it appears to us as a question of boundaries, of determining and delimiting domains. The barrier between life and death, between the living and the nonliving, is set through the insistence of discontinuity and of separated and compartmentalised and delimited substances, ontologies of Being over becoming. Such categorisations are not without their uses; undoubtedly they are necessary in the deployment and successful enactment of a vast number of world views and practices. But what does it cost us to exclude death, the dead and the dying from the spaces of life? What does it cost us to marginalise the nonliving, and claim their absolute exteriority to life? Why do we insist on the thinghood of the dead form and what is the result of this insistence?

So we ask again — "What is death?" and "What is life?" — and it can be clear now that we do not seek a definitive answer, we do not seek a taxonomic explanation of the reductionist kind, just as we do not seek a spiritualistic salvation or transcendence that might appease our anxiety, speak to our ego and promise us the eternity of life; and likewise we do not seek a hylozoism that might make of life all at the expense of making death none. It is perhaps better to be approached as a question of tendencies and fluctuating boundaries, of gradients and transformations, of temporary stratifications and statifications (that is, becoming-static), of continually seeking passages across boundaries that appear to solidify from afar but, as with any solid, become porous and permeable when the scale is changed. With this said and hopefully made clear, it becomes apparent that the questions "What is death?" and "What is life?" no longer hold much weight. It no longer becomes a question of a "what is," of the is-ness of life or death, a question of a determination or a delimitation; but it instead becomes a question of interrogating the formation of the "what is," a challenging of a boundary that common sense appears to hold to be so clear. In this way, we do not seek a universal theory of life and death, but a series of maps, a collation of contingent cartographies, that might better allow us to navigate the numerous tiny deaths, tiny births and tiny lives through which we pass and with which and through which we find connection. There can be no reconciliation at the end, no final answer, and no correct interpretation. We cannot demand of others that they follow us, nor can we uphold the bearings that we might find as correct or true. We can only wayfare and produce what comes to us, with no pretention of universality, generality or finality.

And so, with that, we can now ask not "What is life?" and "What is death?" but where do we find the living and the dead, where do we find them separate and discontinuous, and where do we find them conjoined and in continuity? Where do we find them in a tendential relationship and where do we find this unfolding of the living into the dead, of dying tiny deaths, and this unfolding of the dead into the living, of tiny births and lives, denied? And with this, we can embark and not be held ransom to a dialectical resolution that might deny our wayfaring through the instance of teleology and the final aim. If we are to explore a radically negative anthropology beyond life we cannot have the Absolute Idea or Spirit or One lighting the way, just as we cannot ask of life that it be the principle of the Good and condemn death to the darkened Evil or the void of nihil. What if not only life, but also death, can become an object of tragic affirmation and joy? What if when we dance, we do not dance upon and in spite of the dead, but dance with the dead? How would we write our Hymn to the Night after God's death, and where would we start? Where does that first schism between life and death, that first boundary between the living and the dead, that first demarcation and delimitation between two opposing domains, rest; and one that is "first" not in the sense of universally original or originary, but first only in the sense of our wayfaring?

Finalist-Death, Absolute-Life

At two extremes of a polemic forged by that tradition that declares itself to be Western we find two conceptions of death. Facing one another in what appears to be a mutual exclusion these two notions of death constitute an apparent conflict and opposition. Resting at one end we find the worldly, profane and unspiritual notion of death as belonging to the finitude of bodies, as being the limit of life and its negation. At the other we find a notion of life that escapes death in its promise and assurance of the eternity of the living, the salvation or damnation of the living, in the endless continuation of that which is living upon a plane of life that far exceeds the worldly domain in which we find ourselves immersed.[18] The former notion shall be referred to as telluric-death, from the Latin *tellus* meaning earth, land and ground, and its counterpart in Roman mythology *Terra* — the goddess of the earth. This is a conception of death that would maintain life to be only of the finitude of an individual's earthly body. Beyond the demise of this body, lies death as the empty nothingness and infertile ground of inorganic dust and ashes. Life is constrained to the passage of an individual organism in the world and death is the absolute end-of-life, the zero ground, the forever-encroaching *nihil*. In a pure conception of telluric-death there is no transcendent beyond, no extension of vital duration. Life is immanent to the earthly domain in as much as it dwells within it and never beyond. Beneath is the limit and end-of-life, the outside of life's interior, the nothingness that surrounds and ensures the finitude of life and flesh. *Nihil-death*. The meaning of life is that it dies, and death is *nihil*. This emptiness that *nihil*-death instils in life leaves telluric-death facing two opposing but interrelated options — to surrender and despair to the nothingness and meaninglessness of a life defined by its passage towards death, or the opportunity to grasp hold of this emptiness and mould it, bringing it meaning and worth. Death is either an object of fear and despair, or a great task, burden and opportunity, for the living. Life is all and death is none — death is denied, and life elevated. Death follows life, forever awaiting, forever constraining. The unfolding of life and the passages of the living harbour within themselves the inevitability of their own annihilation and the inescapable assurance of their own finitude.

At the opposing extremity, gazing down upon the earth and here-below, illuminating and darkening, defining and shaping, we find transcendent-death. This conception of death maintains that dying is naught but the passage to a beyond in the sense of a divine plane of continued existence. Eternal-life is the meaning of death and this death is but the blink of an eye through which the finite body is transported to a continuing plane. Earthly-life is made but a shadow of a future truer life — the transcendent plane of heaven and hell or perfect forms from which life draws its meaning and significance. Death is not the limit of life, as it does not truly exist other than as an earthly-death, a profane-death, which is passage to eternal-life. This is the pure transcendent-death. It is a conception of death that also leads us to *nihil*-death, but for contrary reasons.

From continual enshrinements of the tautological definition of death as the negation of life emerges finalist-death. This is the understanding of death that places it in stark opposition to life, as its binary opposite and principle of exclusion. Death becomes the opposite of life, the state of existence devoid of life, the hollow and formless absence that severs the practices of living. Modes of living confront their end in death, and that which is alive is reduced to the negative, sterile and desolate domain of the dead, or death is nothing other than a passing moment enacted upon a fleeting plane of temporality. Death is nothing in the sense of a gnawing zero ground of infertile ashes and dust, or it is nothing for it belongs only to the earthly plane and pertains little to eternity. It is in eternity that true life is located; death is but the judgment day of earthly duration. Life is the absolute determiner of meaning, life finds its meaning in eternal-life, in the Being of the beyond.

The Being of this beyond can be the perfect planes of monotheistic divinity, the absolute Word, but so too can it be the shadow and reflection of earthly-life as in the pantheon of gods. With both, life is absolute, it is eternal and continuing, be it in damnation or salvation. Even if the promise of religious salvation intervenes and turns the horror of death into the promise of eternal life — what remains is a veneration of life, be it celestial, earthly, eternal or finite, and a degradation of death. If death in one world brings about life in another, death is denied. Salvation aims to intervene in the hollowness of death, but in so doing reaffirms it — the domain of the dead becomes the domain of nothingness. Those who are dead are dead, they partake no more in life, or cannot be of life. The dead bury the dead. But also those who are dead are non-existent in the face of life, they are the *nihil* ground, not even an empty stage upon which the drama of life is enacted. The intimacy of life and death is denied, death is subordinated to no more than the illegitimate bastard sibling of life, one so deformed as to not even constitute existing.

But it would be a mistake to think that salvation belongs only to transcendent-death. Salvation manifests itself in the scheme of an apparently telluric-death also, in the promise of meaning being located in a dominant abstract collective — the earthly utopia of the means of production, of scientific progress, of the Cause. Telluric-death reassures the finite individual against the futility of their life through the images of a collectivised-life. One can find meaning in their contribution to telluric utopias, in the collective domain of Spirit that will one day approach a resolution, elevation and end of history. The finite individual can find comfort in the utopias — Art, Culture, Spirit, Progress, Communism, Capital, Rights; the finitude of telluric-life finds salvation given in the teleological significance of future promises. The individual's life is effaced under the image of a continuing life that exists beyond in a series of dominant abstractions that float above the here-below, the here-below being understood as the only space of significance, and yet finding its meaning in the promises of these utopias that are always beyond the individualised-death.

This individualised-death — that is one's ownmost possibility,[19] belonging only to the dead and dying, the death of a certain surface of existential thought — claims to restore to the duration of individuality its ultimate meaning. It is once more a judgment. It is the moment of authentic or inauthentic dying, the utmost unavoidable possibility of life, and the most certain possibility at that. The individualised-death offers the opportunity to grasp hold of death and make it our own, just as the hollowness of life left by telluric-death makes it the bringer of meaning or despair.

Amidst these two — telluric-death and transcendent-death — the figures of absolute-life and finalist-death stand forth, each denying the status of the other. It is not really a case of binary-oppositions, of total mutual exclusions, but of transmutations and translations, of perspectival distortions and interpretations. Telluric-death's veneration of finalist-death so too venerates an absolute-life; just as it declares that death is the inevitable meaning of life, so too does it declare that death is *nihil*, that life is the only space in which the choice of despair or determination is to be made. The spectre of finalist-death folds back and finds its reflection in the image of absolute-life. And likewise, the absolute-life of transcendent-death finds its ever-escaping reflection in an absolute-death reduced once more to the *nihil* ground.

From these transmutations we find ourselves amidst a sea of thanatophobic organologies — systems of organisation where death, the dead, the dying and the nonliving are devalued; that is, made to be objects of negativity and denied their position of connectivity, fluidity and indeed vitality, they are denied the possibility of holding their own meaning beyond the schemes of the living, and so are denied the possibility of becoming objects of tragic affirmation and joy. All becomes interpreted through the scheme of the living, and all that is deemed to be not-of-life is denied.

Salvation seeks to intervene in the scheme of finalist-death, of death as *nihil*. It seeks to ensure the never-ending continuation of the fertility of life, the meaning that life carries, to the domain of dead things. That which has died lives on, in the domain of divine transcendence, or in the earthly abstractions of collectivised-life. One does not die for nothing, one's death finds meaning and purpose in the continuation of life, but it is always from the perspective of the living that this meaning is found. The space of the dead, the domains of the nonliving, are only interpreted through the fruitful perspective of life — the eternal life of the collective, or the eternal life of divinity. Salvation, from the vantage point of the living, deems life as fertile, meaningful and significant, but death is the infertile ground of fear, despair and insignificance.

But in this intervention, in this attempt to give meaning to the dead, salvation hollows out death. Death emerges as an absolute nothingness characterised by emptiness, its meaning only found in life. Death is the outside of life, but one that is so stark a void that it cannot even be declared to be empty. Death as the negation of life has emerged as its outside. In the spaces of the dead, there is nothing. Life judges all, life sees all, and life is the only harbourer of meaning.

An All-Too-Human Soul

What is it that makes the domain of life this fruitful and joyful entity and so banishes the death to nothingness? What is the interior principle that constitutes death as none and life as all? In the emergence of life as the principle of vital interiority, a domain is shaped, a domain of living things that opposes the domain of the dead. The space of life is active and bountiful, whereas its exterior is a gnawing nothingness that is banished from thought and experience. Within the schemes of absolute-life, an interiority is constituted which allows the demarcation of the living in opposition to the dead.

The early atomists considered that the class of those things that manifested movement and sensation were granted these characteristics by soul atoms.[20] These gifts of phenomenological experience and the ability of motion emerged from spherical particles of fire-like soul atoms which, being circular, were best suited to permeate as far as possible. From the motion of these atoms, movement in animals was said to emerge. It was these spheres of fire and soul that permeated Nature, and granted a soulful interior to animality, an interior capable of movement and experience. Their movement compelled life to movement. All that moves is granted movement by these atoms of fire and soul. And perhaps it would in fact be better to here speak not of Nature, but of *phusis*, that primordial gathering and conflict.[21]

For these atomists the only two existent entities, at the most fundamental primordial level, were atoms and void. The atoms, the indivisible final reality, in their spherical fire-soul form, pertain to movement, and it is by the existence of a void, an empty nothingness through which they are able to pass, that their motion is possible. Such an atom is defined by its ability to move through the void, by its autonomy and movement that sets it apart from the void, from non-being, as that which is existent. What we see as moving, and subsequently what we see as living, is a compound collision of these atoms and it is the movement of these atoms that gives them motion and so too sensibility. Thus, Aristotle would state that for these atomists, the soul was that permeation of atoms that brings forth movement.[22] Phenomenological experience, perception and movement emerge from the movements and permeations of these active soul atoms, conjoining mind and soul as to be counted amidst the most primordial of entities. The soul is that which binds body, one for one,[23] and gives it existence and motion. Lucretius writes,

That the principles of body and soul are arranged alternately,
One matching one and so knit the body together.[24]

The soul—the bringer of movement, perception and vitality—is equal to the body, it is conjoined with the body one for one, and it is only with the presence of both in equal measure that we find vitality. Soul permeates matter and conjoins with matter; it is one with the plane of dead things to which it brings life.

In Aristotle the notion of the soul undergoes a transformation that sees it separated from the body. Aristotle too wrote of the soul as being the foundation of life, but contrary to his atomistic and pre-Socratic predecessors he believed that the soul becomes separated from the body and no longer matches and meets it in equality. The soul and matter are no longer entirely entangled entities that move through an infinite series of voids. Instead, the body becomes a carrier of the soul—the body is empty, hollow and dead before it becomes "besouled." [25] The body belongs to the plane of matter, to the plane of unorganized and inactivated potentiality—it is nothing more than an as-yet-shapeless vessel awaiting the form of the soul that may enter it and bring form to the formless. The soul on the other hand belongs to the plane of form and essence, to the transcendent metaphysical plane of actuality, the plane that enters into the Platonic form of the Good. In Aristotle, we do not speak of a thing as living until the form of soul has come to be "in" the body. The soul is not something relative to a body, something entangled with it, something that belongs to the same plane, but rather "it is in a body." [26] The body is but a vessel, a carrier, just as a ship carries its crew. But equally just as a ship would be of little purpose and little use without an embarked crew, so too is the body not living without its soul resting within its interior. The soul becomes the actuality of the body, that which enters into it and makes a living thing, and without it the body degrades and once more becomes dead.

Thus the notion of the soul, and later the subject, enforces the necessity of substance; it creates degrees of being, the soul being of the highest. The metaphysics of substance that results of the soul demeans the world of the dead as the world of the soulless, as the world that has a lesser degree of being and reality. [27] It is the perspective of delimited perception, as belonging to a specific entity labelled here "the soul," that requires a substratum that has lesser reality than it, that is mere matter. The soul is thus not the explanation of the movement of substance, but substance is the result of the soul, it is the substratum of lesser reality that permits the soul to be of the highest reality.

The body that has a soul is living, that which does not is dead and nonliving. But it is not that the body and soul are conjoined entirely just as a ship and its crew are not conjoined entirely; it is not a partnership of one for one, a conjoining of living matter and dead matter in vitality as with the atomists. Rather the soul rests "inside" the body and in so doing brings it life. Without the soul the body returns to the plane of formless matter, to the dead space of the nonliving. Without the soul, the body deforms and degenerates; "when the soul departs the body disintegrates and decays."[28] The soul can "depart," and in so doing condemn the body to the decay and disintegration of death and the dead, for it was the soul that was the bringer of life, and more than that, it is the "first grade of actuality"[29] of a living body, it is its source and cause. Prior to the entering-in of the soul the body was but latent potentiality, for it belonged to the plane of nonliving matter that is without form. Life has become an interior principle, something that enters into a body, rests within a body, and nothing that does not hold this interiority is permitted to enter vitality. The space of life is the space of a soulful interiority, and the boundary between this soulful inside and its outside is the boundary of life and death.

The dead are banished to the exterior of life. These dead entities do not enter into the living practices of nourishment, movement and sensation except as passive entities to be received and incorporated by a living interiority. The active agent is always the living, and the dead are reduced to passive entities, inhabiting a domain that only enters into the space of the living through the action and perspective of the living. The dead are inefficacious and inactive, they are little more than the props and backdrops with which the living engage. Soulless as they are they do not pertain to action, nutrition, sensation, movement or experience, other than at the service of the living, and always from the perspective of life's thinking, perceiving and discriminating interiority.

Within this interiority of life there is a nested hierarchy. The basest of those bodies that have become besouled and so enter the domain of the living are those who possess only the nutritive soul. This caste of soulful living entities would include those beings that appear only to grow and draw nutrition such as most plants. The next soul in this nested hierarchy is the soul that possesses motion, constituting a group that would encompass the majority of animals. Finally, sitting atop this hierarchy we find those entities that possess the noetic soul, the soul that grants the power of thought and reason. This is the domain to which the human, defined famously as the rational animal, belongs as the crowning being of the soulful space of life.

The domain of the living has become a space of efficacy and action. Beyond this domain is an instrumentalised and mechanicalised space of nonliving entities, a space that cannot act, cannot move, and cannot perceive or think. The domain of soulless dead forms only comes to change through the engagement with the living domain, the domain of which the human, possessing the power of thought, is the crowning pinnacle. The power of thought gives the human access to the realm of essences and forms, to the metaphysical space of Truth and reason. It is the human that is the pinnacle of life, and it is life that brings sensation, movement, reason, and so too meaning and purpose, to an otherwise inanimate, formless, instrumentalised domain of nonliving things. There is a rupture and bifurcation between two domains which are posited as opposing and incommensurable, that of the living and the dead.

Transcendent-Life

With this construction of the soul as the interior of life, and an interior that holds access to the plane of True forms and essences at its highest point, the way is paved for the Christian scheme of resurrection and eternal life. Aristotle himself writes that "the soul might even quit the body and re-enter it, and with this would be involved the possibility of a resurrection of animals from the dead." [30] Here the possibility of Christ's resurrection is attested to. The soul is affirmed as being separate to the body once again, not only separate to it in its nature, but also in longevity and importance within the meaningful and active scheme of life. Even a dead body, a body that has lost its life, can rediscover its vitality should the soul return unto it. The soul is eternal, as are the eternal forms and essences of Aristotelean and Socratic thought—the ability to think, belonging to the noetic soul which is the highest representation of the domain of the living, unites the domain of life with the transcendent plane of eternal forms and Truth. This plane as eternal exists beyond the bounds of the earthly, physical, inactive and dead space of the here-below.

This plane of eternal transcendent Truth, to which those bodies occupying the highest point within the hierarchy of the living have access, becomes embodied within the Christian scheme of eternal-life. The eternity of life, the resurrection of Christ, the finding of meaning, Truth and salvation only before God constitutes a form of Platonism for the masses.[31] The soul becomes that entity which takes its vitality from God and returns to truth only before God. The soul that stands before God and gives itself over to God draws closer to the One, to the Truth of the Word.

In Neo-Platonism this soul that constitutes the interiority of life becomes closely associated to a divine monotheistic God, to the One. The soul as the "author of all living things," through divine intervention brings vitality to the "universe of things."[32] This universe of things, of dead, formless and blank matter, is insignificant and inactive prior to the divine permeation of soul; "before the soul, it was stark body—clay and water—or, rather, the blankness of Matter, the absence of Being."[33] The universe of things is nothing but dust and ashes, a space of dead entities devoid of action, perception and agency. This reduction of the domain of the dead and nonliving to an ineffective and inactive space removes it from the scheme of meaning; it is only from the side of the living that meaning exists, and only for the living. The dead are less than dead, reduced to *nihil*.

Within the Christian scheme of eternal-life the only death that can befall a soul is a death that amounts to a continuing of life, but without the illumination of God. As far as the body is concerned, it does not die for it is to all intents and purposes already dead — the departure of the soul from the body constitutes the body's death, but the soul lives on, and was the only reason that the body was said to be living in the first place. For this reason, the body is said to die when life departs it, but that which had life in the first place continues living; the body simply returns to the domain of dust and ashes of which it was always already a part, for it is "mortal and completely bereft of life, and by itself it has no life of any sort."[34] The earthly body always remains within this domain, it is inactive and ineffective, meaningless and powerless unless it is united with a soul, unless it serves as the carrier of a soul.

Equally, the soul comes to lack meaning if it is not united with God, if it does not give itself over to the Word, if it succumbs to that despair that is the sin of the denial of the Lord.[35] The soul "never entirely ceases to live"[36] for it belongs to that eternal plane of transcendence, which finds its earthly pinnacle in Man, and its transcendent meaning in God. A soul that does not unite itself with God befalls a "second death,"[37] but it is a form of death that remains in life but without the Lord. Augustine writes of this death as "dying for all eternity."[38] The soul enters a domain of life that is characterised by torment and pain, but it remains a domain of life, it is not the space of dust and ashes to which the body remained bound.

This scheme of transcendent-life reduces death to nothing. It is a meaningless and bland backdrop upon which the game of vitality, here including only the living, is enacted. The domain of the nonliving and dead, which here comes to include the body which is but a carrier for the living and active soul, is reduced to a certain ground of nothingness, a nothingness based in nihilism and emptiness. The nonliving are banished from the schemes of that which is meaningful, that which has purpose, and that which is capable of thought and action. Life is defined in relation to divinity, in relation to transcendence, to a plane of eternity and continuing existence that separates itself from the temporal and degrading domain of the here-below.

The Arrogance of Man

It would be tempting to declare that after the death of God the devaluation of the dead that transcendent-life enacts is resolved, and that the apparent domination of the scheme of telluric-death which echoes the Epicurean declaration that death is no impingement on the living, and finds articulation in the existential individualised-death, resolves the veneration of an eternal-life and confronts death for what it is. In the scheme of telluric-death, there is no more transcendence to a plane of eternal-life. But it is in part this echo of the declaration that "death is nothing to us"[39] which causes the scheme of telluric-death to enact the same reduction of death to an empty nothingness.

What is more, the separation of the domains of the living and the dead continues in schemes of telluric-death. Life and death continue to be separate from one another, as states of being kept apart by a barrier that continues to create an inside of life that is endlessly pursued by its mortified exterior. But whilst it is endlessly pursued by this outside, it does not permit it to enter into tendential connection with it. The world of life, of which Man is the crowning being, continues to act as the active interior. I use the capitalised masculine expression "Man" critically as it is a further element in the separation, hierarchisation, and formation of a dominant abstraction that denies entry to the highest pinnacle of life to any who do not meet the masculine marks of normativ-

41

ity.[40] In this separation, Man continues to act as master of the domain of the living, and the bringer of meaning to the domain of the dead. This arrogance that places Man atop the world, and subordinates the lesser living and the inactive dead to Man's efficacy, sees the formation of the *Gottmensch*, the God-Man, which is the basis of humanism. It is Man,

> who by the strength of his organization, and the power of his intelligence, is brought into communion with all nature; is lord and ruler of all living beings on the earth; who, turning his eyes towards heaven, studies the laws which govern the motions of the stars, and contemplates them in the infinite space; who has measured and weighed the mass of the terrestrial globe and of the spheres revolving around; man, who calculates the speed of light, and traces, through centuries, the motions of that imponderable fluid; who, multiplying the power of his organs, has acquainted himself with myriads of beings unperceived by his senses; and has discovered in the depth of space innumerable suns rolling beyond the reach of his unassisted sight; man, who, rapt in his ideas and meditating upon himself, regulates the inward movements of his imagination and dares to consider his mind as a brilliant ray of the supreme and omnilatent light reflected in living and sentient creatures; man, whose species grows and developes itself as a unique being incessantly advancing towards a perfection to which no limit can be assigned; whose speculations embrace the origin of things and the principle of his own existence.[41]

The schism that separated the living from the dead, and in turn placed the rational animal atop of the hierarchy of the living, continues in the scheme of telluric-death. Man becomes master of the universe, and follows the flight of the gods by installing his own image in their place. With the domain now labelled "Nature" sufficiently mechanised and externalised, Man becomes the only meaningful entity, the explainer of all.

Thus Man sets itself apart from the world that it inhabits, as superior and utterly different. Consciousness, Spirit, Soul, Mind — all these notions have separated the human from the world of things, those things that are animalistic or nonliving. In this schema the human has made itself master of a world entirely devoid of continuity. It is the meaning-giving rupture that breaks the world into the social-cultural, meaning-laden world of people as the pinnacle of life and existence, and the empty, hollow, mechanical world of things. The human is not an object, but the perceiver and creator of all objects; for without the human subject, endowed as it is with Mind, Spirit and Soul, there is no object for perception or consideration. It is in this way that the human has denied the fact that it is but one thing among other things, it is but one part of a continuity, but one part of a world that would not blink for a second were it to be removed. Thus is created a world of things, things-at-hand, and of use and utility, a strictly functional reality, to which life, and most importantly human life, brings meaning and purpose. The barrier of the subject and object splits human life from the world that defines it, but does so illusorily.

When we try to consider the world as an external world of things, when we deny it continuity and equality, all we can find in it is the reflection of ourselves, of our thought and our being; we find it as a domain of substance of lesser reality. We interpret this as the sign that we are the bringers of meaning to an otherwise insignificant state of affairs, but what is the reflection that we are faced with if it is not the reverberation of an infinite echo of the impossibility of limits, of the impossibility of determining the outside of objects and the inside of subjects? We claim that this is our projection of meaning, our expression of Spirit, but from where would this meaning and Spirit emerge if not from continuity with that which is claimed as objectified, instrumentalised and functionalised? The inside — the subject, life, Spirit — and the outside — the object, utility, function — have never been more than stubborn confusion, an inability to recognise the mist as mist, the porous as porous, the continuous as continuous. The divinity of God springs forth in this mist and by projecting the centres of meaning — Spirit, Consciousness, Soul — finds itself amidst the world of things, not in enchanting, but in divining. The arrogance of Man, believing that it is the bringer of meaning, finds for itself the authority to explain the efficacy of the world that it has functionalised. This Supreme Being, this entity that explains the meaning of the meaningless, the *Gottmensch*, cannot be more than an impoverishment and disenchantment of the true richness of the world, emerging as it does from a denial of continuity and from an inability to recognise mist as mist.

What this arrogance reveals is "the *hyperbolic naïveté* of man: positing himself as the meaning and measure of the value of things." [42] This naïveté seeks to separate out the interiority of life from the world that it inhabits, and in so doing grants itself a position of privilege amongst all. Perspectives of the other are denied, and Man, the supposedly highest representation of a divine life, becomes the only entity capable of bringing meaning to an otherwise hollow and void world. Shrouding itself in a mist of absolutism, stratification and statification, this arrogance enacts a form of judgment on the world, a judgment of God, a judgment in which Man becomes the court, the ruler and sovereign. All else is condemned to inefficacy and meaninglessness, only capable of being brought to light by the illuminating gaze of the being that knows.

In this way, all other living beings are denied entry to the pinnacle of life, "they are something, not somebody." [43] And thus unfolds a gaping void between Man and its world, a void which demeans both the world and the beings which declare themselves to be Man, for their continuity with the world, their dwelling in life and death, is concealed and denied. It is not simply a problem of faculties; "the problem is not human beings' denying something to other critters — whether that be language, or knowledge of death, or whatever is the theroetico-empirical sign of the Big Gap popular at the moment — but rather the death-defying arrogance of ascribing such wondrous positivities to the Human."[44] Man is life. And what is more, it is a life possessing an essentialised noetic soul that may persist for eternity in unchanging form, in salvation or damnation, and in a form devoid of the transformation that is integral to becoming and connection. Standing before the world, Man erects a fortress of interiority — a fortress that on closer inspection is nothing but mist — and on the opposing side of this fortress stands a domain of static, formless, and inactive matter, a domain of death devoid of connection to life.

The Durative-Soul

But what if the soul were not the prerequisite of substance? What if it were not that meaningful substance that stratifies all else below it? What if it were not that which finds its highest representation in the form of Man, in a hyperbolic naiveté and arrogance? What if it were not that which sits above and beyond lesser substances? What if it were not immortal but durative? What if it were not of mind, but body? And what if it were not that which entered "into" dead matter and brought meaning and life to an otherwise dead and ineffective domain?

Aristotle asks two questions which, to him, appear absurd. They appear absurd because the soul has already been posited as the bringer of experience and movement, the bringer of meaning. Aristotle has already separated the soul from other substance as the Life of the living. He asks,

> If, on the other hand, the points of the body are identical with the
> units whose number is the soul, or if the number of the points in
> the body is the soul, why have not all bodies souls?[45]

and secondly,

> Who would suggest that stone or man could enter into the
> constitution of the soul?[46]

Why do not all bodies have souls? Why do the dead entities not
have souls? They fall outside the Life of the living; they do not
enter into the interior strata of life. But what if a soul were not a
different kind of substance than the body; what if it in fact was
the body? Would it still then be a soul? Perhaps not, but for the
sake of expression we will retain the word—not in a divine essentialist form or sense, but in the sense of the singularity of each
entity and its passages of becoming.

Such a soul, a durative-soul, which could perhaps also be called
a mortal-soul[47] or apparently contradictorily a bodily-soul, is a
notion that resonates to some extent with the soul as the body's
clinamen, as the Lucretian swerve of an atom,[48] the movement of
a singular entity, the passages of bodies and individualities. This
soul would be the inscription of a body's movement and duration. It is not an entity separate to the body, but is the trace of
its movement, the accumulation and swelling of its duration and
connection. In this way, it is not separate to the body, it is not
the essence of a *res cogitans*, a thinking substance, it is not the
immaterial counterpart to a material body, but the specific singular duration through which a body travels. This duration cannot
help but extend beyond the physical limits of a given body, but
that does not mean that it is other than it—it is the trajectory of
that body's formation and the continual influence that specific

duration holds with other bodies. That is to say, it is both effective and affective in presence and absence, beyond the birth and degradation of a body, beyond that given body's life and death. It demands a place in futures through its swelling and determination, but also in pasts through its being determined and its interpretive expansion, that is the recalling of the past in the formation of presents and futures.

This durative-soul is, as we have said, not an opposition to the body; rather the body enters into the duration and formation of this soul, and it is one of the many recording surfaces from which duratively singular but extensively multiple connection and interaction emerges. Every event through which a body passes is recorded in some way, not only in the noetic and conceptual patterns within which that body is immersed, but in the tightness of the muscles, in the flinching of the body, in the reactions of the gut, in the scar tissues that form upon the skin's surface, in the haptic memory that we form through habit, and further in the formations and patterns of a vast range of nonhuman entities — in basalt columns, in the leaning of a tree in the wind, in the formation of stalagmites within caverns, in the fossilisation of the remnants of the dead. It is this singular duration of recording and formation and its contemplation that constitutes these souls and the unique collection of retentions and protentions that, temporarily, find expression within a body but are not limited to it. It is not an immutable essence, but an ever-changing singular duration, and one which is not bound, but continually undoes itself, recreates itself, and finds endless intersections in the becoming of the between, an element of the emergence of difference and will through the eternal return. It is less the origin of movement but more that which is emergent of the interaction, connection and entanglement of movement — the singular, and yet at the same time multiple, durations through which habit, memory and form are made. Singular, for it is incommensurable, irreducible and untranslatable—an ever-changing nomadic monad. Multiple, for it is emergent of the most varied and heterogeneous connections and intersections; a monad that, apparently paradoxically, from another perspective appears composite.

Such a soul grants bodies power of action. Not in the sense of some kind of immaterial essentialist interiority, or an internal will, agency or vitalist force, but in the sense that it is the specific contexts and durations in which a body is immersed that allow it to act in a certain way, that determine it as it continually seeks to move beyond such determinations. It is a soul that is determined and yet still finds space for determination. It is not some kind of metaphysical, anthropocentric agency, but the inscription of the connections, interactions and durations in which a body engages—it is what allows a body to do that which it can do. It is what allows a body to move, develop and transform, in spite of the determination of the milieus in which it find itself immersed. In this sense the soul is the inscription of a body's ethics, it is the recording surface of its *ars vitae* and so too its many deaths.

This does not mean however that this soul, in the manner by which we are here describing it, is limited to a body. On the contrary, it continually overspills the limits both of itself, and the body. It is caught in connections that exceed the limits of bodies, as demonstrated by the unhealable scars, and continual sources of inspiration that we find from those once living beings who have now passed, for the most part, into death. This durative-soul is both phenomenological and naturalistic. One means of explanation does not exclude the other.

This type of soul, then, if indeed it can still be described as a soul, is not limited to humans, or even animals. The formation of the rocks upon which we stand, the clouds which pass above us, the water in which we bathe, all have singular durations which are in endless networks of interaction and affection from which emerges an infinite proliferation of multiple connections. And in this proliferation the nothingness that is the beyond labelled as "death" becomes no longer *nihil* but *infinitum*. It is no longer an emptiness that is a nihilistic void, but a nothingness that is unlimited in the sense that its proliferation defies limits of a given entity and dissolves the inside. We only need to look at the layers of rock formations studied by geology to find a recording surface of a supposedly dead soul, just as we need only pick up certain rocks from the beach, made smooth by years and years of tumbling amidst water, to see the marks of the singular duration that has led to their formation. And these formations enter into effective and affective interaction with countless others, granting the conditions of other formations, of other durations, and other connections—a determination that is also determined, a paradox of will within a deterministic world.

Thales suggests such an interpretation of the soul, not as the essence of a stratified being, nor as the Life of the living, when he describes the magnet as possessing a soul due to its ability to move iron; however, with him it appears to be movement that remains the foundational characteristic. With this durative-soul it is not that movement no longer has a place in it, quite the contrary; rather, it is that the durative-soul is emergent of the interaction and affection of movement. It remains continuous with movement, whilst being different from it.

Is the soul then a finite mode of an infinite substance that negotiates the movements between finitude and infinity? As Spinoza writes, "the human mind cannot be absolutely destroyed with the body, but something remains which is eternal." [49] That is, it remains entangled with the infinite. This is not the eternity of the mind as the immaterial and sacred counterpart of the material and profane body but rather is the necessary continuation of singular connection. It is not the continuation in immaterial form of a material *res cogitans*, but an emergence of sovereign individuality through a process of individuation by which multiplicity creates singularity, creating that which is unique and monadic from the intersection of a whole host of entities and processes. That which was extended and connected does not cease to be so with the demise of a body—its singular affect remains and continues to grow and swell. In this way, the body, as soul, is eternal in affection and connection, in its continual thrust into the future and its reinterpretation and contemplation of the past, its continual returning of pasts in presents and futures. It is the interaction and effective accumulation of events that, as Proust writes, "are larger than the moment in which they occur and cannot be entirely contained in it... they overflow into the future... [and] demand a place also in the time that precedes them."[50] This is a continuation into a beyond that denies the linearity of finite temporality whilst remaining immanent to the passages of becoming. It does not aim at a beyond that would be transcendent, but would be that infinite nothingness that lies beyond the perceived limits of a being,[51] that denies the permeability of such limits, and affirms individuality, multiplicity and difference in connection.

This is an infinitude which belongs to all-things—it gives us not the comfort of an anthropocentric afterlife in which our immaterial form continues after the demise of our body's material existence, but gives us, and all-things, eternity in relation to the infinite, that is in connection, that nothingness that is the beyond of any given entity. Here we are brought to an affirmation of the eternal return as the contingent and tireless recurrence of infinite difference that ensures both the repetitive and the new, the boundless dice throw which enforces the necessity of chance[52] and the emergence of difference through repetition. This eternity is the recurrence and continuation of singular and specific ratios of motion and rest.

This is one means of reading the Spinozan category of the *adequate idea* in the *Short Treatise*. Here, the more we attain of adequate ideas, the more we are able to grasp hold of our connection to the eternal and infinite — we see the necessity of contingency, the necessity of the demise of that which is good, we come to learn to live and die through a jubulant *amor fati*,[53] a love of fate. We are able to participate in eternity and grasp hold of our place within connection. This is what Proust sees in the work of art as escaping a finalist-death — the grasping and expressing of an adequate idea allowing us to approach our relationship to that which is not finite, that which is infinite, that which is beyond, that which surpasses itself. And this is what makes the great work of art "timeless": its expression of an adequate idea that communicates something of our relation to the infinite. In this way, as we grasp adequate ideas and our relation to the eternal, infinite and possible, "the less death is harmful to us"[54] for our being partakes in its connection to the eternal. This is a doctrine not of the immortality of the personal soul, nor an anthropocentric continuation of the ego after death, but of the necessity of partaking in an eternal return of the infinite — this is a relation to death, to the after-of-life, to the nonliving, which escapes the grasp of finalism. It is an extension of a soul as modification that has "its origin in the body" and as such "depends on the body alone."[55] And this is not just a stratified body and an anthropocentric soul, but of "all the infinite attributes which have a soul as well as extension."[56]

The movement, swelling and multiple formation of these durative-souls then, is that of a continual going-beyond, a going-beyond that is always beyond and has never arrived, not a beyond that is transcendent or divine, but a beyond of connection and interaction, a receding horizon. It is precisely the movement that defies barriers, that defies staticity and shatters the enclosed. In its going-beyond of itself it is always surpassing itself, it is always communicating, always exchanging and changing. The arrival of an absolute Spirit, the resolution of contradiction in thought, would be its end. The very beyond to which it continually extends its reach would vanish, its horizon would cease to be a horizon. It is this arrival of the limit that cannot be thought without the normativity that would raise repetition beyond the difference to which spirit and soul would reach; it is this arrival of limit that cannot occur. The arrival of the limit, of the absolute Idea, would be the annihilation of the multiplicity of durative-souls—effacement under the unifying normativity and nihilism of the One, the reduction to stratifications of substance. This arrival of a limit that is sought in dialectic resolution would then be the denial of the tendential continuity of life and death, the denial of the heterogeneity, multiplicity and connectivity of durative-souls.

Dead Thought, Living Death

So we return once more to our initial questions. Again not expressed in terms of the is-ness of death and the is-ness of life, not pertaining to the essences of states of being, but to the positing of the tendential continuity of the living and the dead, to the exchange and interaction of the nonliving and the living. What becomes of life in its passage into death? And inversely, what becomes of the nonliving in its passage towards life? Put simply—do the dead live, and in what ways are the living dead? What becomes of the domains of life and death when they are no longer posited as oppositional states, but as processes that unfold towards one another and continually permeate one another?

With the durative-soul laid before us as a proliferation of multiple singularities, of unique passages of connections and intersections, the questions take on new complexities and shades. No longer can a barrier be erected, on one side of which stand the dead and *nihil* and on the other side the living and *infinitum*; rather we find the relationship of the living to the dead to be precisely that of *infinitum* to the extent that even nothingness is no longer characterisable as *nihil*. There is one sense then in which the question of death is the question of the infinite, the question of the relation of finitude to infinity. What becomes of a finite body, a mortal being, in its unfolding to that which is beyond it, to the infinite domain of connection and potentiality?

This too is in some respects a question of the noetic capacities of the living, of the experience of individualised consciousness; the question of the relation of that which is experienced as the isolated, separated subjectivity of the individual to that which lies beyond it, that which it can never fully approach. The durative-soul and its undoing of the hyperbolic naïveté of Man does not deny the significance of that which is experienced as individual consciousness, of the articulation of subjectivity that we experience in some sense as self and perception, but rather reminds us of its transient, contingent and interdependent nature. The experience of consciousness, of *noesis*, is not some kind of divine intervention, but is precisely borne of the intersection and proliferation of durative-souls; that is, it is entirely continuous with the material domains of the nonliving and is one particular articulation of these interactions and intersections. As the flows of durative singularities collide, further individualities emerge, and the situatedness of consciousness stands amidst these collisions, positioned in such a way that it's left unable to fully grasp the beyond of the horizon that is integral to any position. Consciousness stands in a network of the living and the dead, and it is precisely this standing that means it constitutes a horizon, just as when one stands in any given position and looks outwards limits to vision are ascribed by the specificity of that very position.

So it is not a question of whether the dead think like us, for the singularity of our positions deny that anything, even the other, should think like us. Rather the question is about the continuity of networks that lead to and form a part of thinking in the first place. With the divinity of the Word and the creator removed from the equation, the experience of consciousness becomes an emergence, an affect, an entity resultant of the collision and intersection of other entities — both living and dead — and yet distinguishable from those other entities of which it is formed and with which it is continuous whilst being distinct. That consciousness is a unique experience should not be denied, but that does not necessarily leave us in a situation where the only explanation is one of transcendence, of an eternal soul and divine light. Rather we can acknowledge the continuity of this singular consciousness with that which, from its limited position and perspective, it is not.

So do the dead think? Here, it is not a matter of ascribing limits to thought, of declaring this or that to hold the faculty of *noesis*, but rather a matter of beginning to grasp as best we can from our limited position the continuities of matter that allow for thought to be a possibility in the first place. These are some of the questions approached and opened by biosemiotics, the study of the exchange of signs in the biological domain, and the field's acknowledgement, albeit here through the limitations of semiotics, that it is not only the human that exchanges signs. The implication of this acknowledgement should become larger than the domain of the sign, revealing that also it is not only the human that enters into the chains of subjectivity.

This is a form of distributed subjectivity in which the individual consciousness is but one articulation of a chain and network that extends well beyond it and which makes its articulation possible in the first place. It is an ontology that allows for the singularity of experience, whilst also acknowledging its continuity, and which reforms the question — do the dead think? — to take on a totally different meaning, for no longer is the notion of the thinking dead dependent on the possession of a noetic living soul; rather the notion of the thinking dead is quite simply an acknowledgement of the continuity of what we experience as subjectivity with the material world. That the dead do not think like us appears obvious, but then not even the other—human or nonhuman—thinks like us, for we cannot help but occupy certain positions, more homogenous or more heterogeneous at differing points. But that the dead think, in a manner entirely different to us, appears clear for it is the thought of the nonliving, of the entities prior to individual birth and following the processes of dying, that form in intersection that which is experienced as one's consciousness. Thus the notion of *res cogitans* holds meaning, but no longer in distinction to *res extensia*, for it is the fact that matter contemplates and results in emergence that allows for the experience of consciousness in the first place. This is seen on the micro scale by the numerous nonhuman entities that form and inhabit the human body and which reveal it on closer inspection to be an assemblage of forms of life that are other than human.

In the same way, the question of the continuation of life, that in the scheme of transcendent-life was found as salvation and eternal life, becomes redefined. It is not the matter of the transference of an essentialist and unchanging soul continuing in the same form and merely departing from an earthly inhabitation, as though the same unchanging soul finds new spaces of dwelling. Rather than being a question of the eternity of an unchanging soul, the question of the life of the dead is a question of transformative continuity; it is not a question of transcendent eternity, but of the association of the finite to that which is infinite, to that which lies beyond it. So we do not ask "Do the dead live on?," as though there is simply a transference of the Life of the living in the form of the bounded soul to another plane or vessel, but we instead approach the continuity of the experience of life to the experience of death and of the role played by the nonliving in the articulation of life. So the dead do live on and cannot be buried, but this does not grant an essentialised soul eternal life. It is an after-of-life without it being an afterlife, for the passage of a being in the world, the imprints and traces made in the intersection of durative-souls, cannot be undone and the reverberations are felt in domains which far exceed individualised articulation and experience, falling well beyond the horizon of its position.

So the deadness of the dead is a deadness of individualised experience, but in this death the passage of life remains active beyond individualised degradation. Whilst this is not a matter of the continuation of individualised consciousness as it is experienced in the domain of individualised-life, of the existential self, neither is it only a matter of material effect and its continuation. To separate out the subjective from the material, matter from thought, is to fail to apprehend the significance of the tendential continuity of the living and the dead; it is to fail to acknowledge the continuity of matter and thought, and the heterogeneity of thinking matter. It would be to reaffirm the arrogance of Man that declared itself to be the only entity capable of possessing the noetic soul. This is the significance of Spinoza's *Deus sive Natura* (God or Nature), which conflates divinity and materiality challenging the transcendence of the former in the process; Nietzsche's characterisation of will as a fundamental force of ontology, not of Being but of becoming; Tarde's nonhuman societies and collations of monads; and Deleuze and Guattari granting desire to entities beyond the human — namely that what we experience as our own will, our own desire, our own thought, and our own life, is an articulation of an interplay of forces that far exceed the horizon of our perspectives, that we are articulations of intersections that go beyond us, beyond life, and undo the boundedness that our experience presents us with. To distribute subjectivity, agency, desire and will is also to distribute life, not in a way that denies the singularity of experience or affect, but acknowledges that experience as being formed of intersections which are far from bounded and cannot be fully apprehended from the position of bounded subjectivity. This is the chaos in which we find the subject articulating itself, the space of extensive connection from which stands forth individual phenomenological experience, and to which it returns endlessly, not only at the point of its grand Death, but also repetitively as it unfolds and travels through an entire constellation of tiny deaths.

CHAPTER 2

Dissolutions of Insides

Subjects, Objects and the World of Things

The division of the world into subjects and objects is one of the most well-trodden paths of philosophical debate. We will not tire ourselves by returning along this worn-down path other than when absolutely necessary for our purpose at hand. There is little to be gained from marching faithfully and respectfully through the history of monumental proper nouns, of the formation of these two entities, that has not already been gained by others elsewhere. What concerns us here is the efficacy of the living over the dead and how the division of the world into subjects and objects has enacted and reinforced this claimed efficacy.

The creation of an interior to life that thinking through the soul initiated finds its continuation in the notion of the subject. Once again we here find the human form, or more appropriately that of Man, resting at the top of a stratified hierarchy of the living. The subject is that entity which possesses the character-istics of the rational soul, the elements of perception, thought and reason. For this reason, the subject is the source of meaning in the world for only it is possessive of the faculties of conscious-ness. The subject separates itself out from the world, and its exte-rior becomes the domain of mere objects, of nonliving, inactive and ineffective entities that populate the outside of the subject.

A barrier is erected between an interiority of the subject, and the extensive domain that lies beyond them, a barrier so power-ful as to isolate the subject behind the "veil of Mâya"[57] that has been reinterpreted and reconstituted through a metaphysics of substance. The soul of Aristotle, that active interiority that brings life to otherwise inanimate dead matter, rises again in the non-corporeal substance of *res cogitans*. And just as the soul entered into the body, devoid of life, so too for the subject the body is "merely an extended, non-thinking thing."[58] The interiority of the subject is so radically veiled from the externality of objects that it alone becomes entirely certain of its existence, and its continuity with bodies is an object of doubt. The object can never be trusted to exist for it is only the manifold interiority of the subject that can be certain to have reality. The domain of the nonliving, the domain of objects, does not enter into the interiority of the subject and mind; thought and existence are linked and isolated. The void that lies beyond the subject can never be perceived or experienced. The soulful interiority of life is radically distinguished from all else to the extent that it becomes an isolated phenomenon.

With one of the founding statements of his pragmatic anthropology, Kant reaffirms the stratified hierarchy of the subject through the assertion that the human sense of self, the ability to say "I," "raises him infinitely above all other living beings on earth."[59] Going further, Kant declares that the human is "through rank and dignity an entirely different being from *things*, such as irrational animals, with which one can do as one likes."[60] It is the ability to say "I" and the sense of self and anthropocentric personhood that this is said to imply that raises the human above all-things. It is the interiority of the subject that separates that subject from the world. There is a further entrenchment of the schism between the interior of life and its exterior, an interior of life which at its pinnacle can say "I" and an exterior of that subject that is populated only by "*things*."

Life, and in particular its pinnacle of human life, is characterised by a sensuous and reasoning interiority, and the domain of the nonliving, and indeed of death, is characterised by a lack. It is a lack of thought, a lack of sensation, a lack of experience, which characterises the nonliving and the dead. In this vein Kant declares that "*unconsciousness*... is a foretaste of death."[61] Unconsciousness, and the lack of experience and phenomenology that it implies, presents an image of the domain of the dead, a domain that is devoid of thought and sensation. The passage to death, here suggested in unconsciousness, is a passage from an active interiority to a nihilistic exteriority; it is a passage from Self, from I, to Other, to mere "*things*" and "objects." The subject, isolated from any place or connectivity, is closed in upon itself, and to undo this closure can only mean death, can only mean entry to a nihilistic void, a space of finalist-death.

This entrenchment of an interior/exterior split leads to some peculiar consequences. Not only does it produce a normalised subject that appears as distinct from the world, it goes further and produces a worldless subject.[62] It produces an interior of the subject, the master of the living and its highest representation, which cannot gain access to anything exterior to it. To access this exterior is to stare into a void that in staring back reduces the subject to nothingness. To seek to journey beyond the subject's limits, to access the domain of "*things*," is to stare at death; it is to gaze beyond the limits of the subject's being and as such dissolve into a domain of nonexistence. But what is the nothingness that lies beyond the veil that surrounds the subject? What exists outside of the domain of that entity that can say "I"? Is it not precisely the exterior which comes to form the interior? And is there not a continual interplay, a continual communication, which creates an inside? Is the inside not produced by means of the outside and the outside through inside to the extent that their clear demarcation becomes an impossibility, an absurdity? What is the nothingness, the dead domain, which lies beyond experiential interiority?

The interpretation of nothingness is a crucial moment. It can become the total pitfall, leading to a gnawing nihilism that devours any attempt at active thought. This is one way to understand Nietzsche's oft-referenced abyss that stares back[63] — not that the world is nothingness, not a helpless despair, but a warning that if one stares at a nihilistic nothingness, if one makes nihilism, then nihilism will stare back, it will devour all. Nihilism is infectious. But the beyond that we encounter in the world that is concealed from the delimited subject by the veil of Mâya, that presents it with a nihilistic image of finalist-death, need not be characterised by nihilism. Rather, following Bataille,[64] it can merely be that domain of the beyond, the space which exists beyond the perceived limits of a being, the creative, necessary and active domain of continuity and continual communication that in its constant turmoil produces the limits of self, of the I, of the apparent subject, as transient and instable boundaries, that enforces the worldliness of beings and denies the barrier between I and Other. This is that nothingness that is *infinitum*, that is the proliferation of singular multiplicity and durative-souls of an endlessly recurring becoming with no object other than itself.

With Bataille we find the combination of modernist and enlightenment concepts — the object, the subject — and the surrealistic space of contradiction and confusion. In Bataille, reality is rupture, war and contradiction; as Sartre wrote, it is conflict.[65] The integral confusion, which Bataille himself acknowledged,[66] that comes with his thought reflects the impossibility of thinking discontinuous entities such as subjects, objects, insides, outsides and bounded individuals through the lens of continuity and connection, and through those points of continuity that most disgust us due to their ability to force us to recognise this continuity — death, sex, defecation. In Bataille, the theory of the subject and object unfolds as a surrealistic nightmare, the enforced separations and discontinuities of which rob us of our subjective sovereignty whilst demeaning us to the objective *world of things* that places becoming at the service of some teleology, some object other than its own, some monism of purpose or utility.

There is a primordial continuity in Bataille, where the living and the dead not only unfold unto one another but at times become inseparable from one another, where the individual and self dissolve amidst a continuous reality that equally continually forces itself apart into bound entities which, no sooner than they are bound, once again dissolve in powerful communication. The living and the dead, whilst different kinds of entities, are continuous; "death is that putrefaction, that stench... which is at once the source and the repulsive condition of life."[67] The moral order reels in the face of death, for it presents it with the undoing of its union of subjects. The subject and object become elements of discontinuity that in their refusal to recognise their communicative continuity oppress subjectivity and reduce it to the order of the *world of things*. This *world of things* is produced from the perspective that would insist upon the stratification, statification and compartmentalisation of all, would insist upon their utility and function, that would be a principle of functional reality with which "one can do as one pleases." It would demand of each entity its classification and separation from the continuities of the world. It would subject each entity to a determination that degrades it, placing it in the service of another cause, a cause that is not active and self-determining but reactive and determined—at the cause of a beyond that is not the beyond of extensive communication, but the beyond of the transcendental power, of the transcendent-death, of the upstanding subject, of the accumulative power of capital. The *world of things* is that domain that the perspective of the worldless isolated subject creates in its denial of continuity, it is separation of substance into hierarchised departments, in the insistence of a metaphysics of substance that is unable to cope with continuity and connectivity.

The subject, compartmentalised and functionalised from a position of exteriority, becomes integrated to a servile world of things where "it has no meaning other than its material qualities, adapted or not to some useful purpose, in the productive sense of the word."[68] In spite of all the anthropocentric arrogance of the subject, it too becomes reduced to the level of objects as it folds back on itself, becoming integrated into an objective reality which from the position of exteriority causes the inside of life to appear as the dead outside. The perspective of *the world of things*, which reduces subjects to objects and puts them to the service of a being outside of becoming, degrades subjective sovereignty and makes it servile. The inside of life is folded out of itself and enters into that domain of *nihil*-death where it is but an object. The naïveté that ascribed a superior interiority to the pinnacle of Life undoes itself as even interiority comes to perceive itself in functional, objectified terms. A locus of contradiction emerges where that which claims to be subject appears to even itself as object.

The subject, worldless and taxonomised, legislated and judged, now emerges as a shattered entity, the sovereignty of its durative-soul denied, compartmentalised and put to the service of teleological causes. Perspectives of utility, of objects, become constructed to increase the power of the human subject's domination, of the superiority of the subject, through the principles of a functional reality and a world of things. The projection of human arrogance and hyperbolic naïveté, of life's pinnacle, is mapped onto a devalued, nihilistic domain of ineffective dead objects. The *res cogitans* of Descartes should be a kind of substance distinct from other forms of substance,[69] that is it should be the thinker of what is thought. It is that I-saying substance that in thinking can do with objects "as it pleases." The act of thinking becomes separated from that which it is "thinking about," and the veil of Mâya, in the sense of the barrier that separates the subject from its world, is reinforced by the notion of substance. There should be a thinking substance that is separate, superior and in fact enclosed from other substances which are mere items to be given up to thought, which are servile, and which even the subject becomes, from the position of the externality foreshadowed in unconsciousness and promised by death. "What Descartes desired was that thought should have, not an *apparent* reality but a reality in itself." [70] The *res cogitans* is the demand of an absolute reality for the thinking matter of the subject, a reality that reduces all else, and so by extension itself, to nihilism.

Selfhood

This conflict that the shattering of the world into objects and subjects resting upon the substratum of substance reiterates is echoed in a different tonality in Nishida Kitarō's[71] notion of the self as a locus of absolute contradiction. In Nishida the self emerges as a space of intersection between finitude of an individual entity and the infinite world of continuity. It is a space of paradox in which finitude and infinity converge and the sensation of "I" dissolves back into the bottomless depths of its formation and existence. As Dōgen writes, "to study the self is to forget the self." [72] To examine what appears as interiority, is to reveal the impossibility of maintaining the boundary that surrounds the inside. Such continuity does not just transcend individuals, but concerns the very basis of their existence. That life, paradoxically, opens up unto death and death unto life is the condition of the bottomless and tendential communication of both; that the self opens up unto the other is the condition of its existence. As Nishida writes, "the existential self discovers the self-transforming matrix of its own bottomless depths. It discovers that it is born from history, is active in history, and dies to history." [73] The sense of self is formed by a nothingness that is not *nihil* but *infinitum*, it is formed in its continual unfolding unto that which is other than it, and it is formed of this intensive contradiction.

It would be a mistake to ascribe this viewpoint to ascetic mysticism. The dissolution of self is not a mystical movement but in many respects a realist and materialist one; it is the refusal of the normalised self and subject and the compartmentalisation this implies; it is a refusal of total determination and delimitation. Not only that, it is recognition of the formation of interiority

65

by exteriority, of the transient nature of boundaries. Reflection upon the selfhood that Kant's I-saying subject implies cannot help but reveal the impossibility of maintaining the I as an isolated and worldless interiority. The unfolding of interiority into the world of things is revealed. The isolated I-sayer, perceived from a position of externality that is adopted even by the self that says this I, becomes an object, a functionalised "thing." The enforcement of the barrier between the living interior and the objectified exterior results in the degradation of both.

This externality that is fundamental to interiority, and the transformation of the subject to an object that the separation necessitates, is in one sense revealed by Lacan's mirror stage,[74] which denies the autonomy and isolation of subjective interiority instead revealing it as extensive and transformative in communication. The self, the I-saying entity, the ego, is revealed in the mirror stage to be formed precisely in relation to that which is not I, the subject becomes through objects. It is the recognition of that which is other than I that forms I, and forever ensures the shattering of the unified ego. It is the interrelated formation of *innenwelt* through *umwelt*, of inner-worlds through outer-worlds, of the formation of the I through the not-I, to the point that this communication "tips the whole of human knowledge into mediatization through the desire of the other" and so makes it a structure of being-there and subjectivity—the demand to adhere to an I-ness, a Self, becomes alienating and oppressive in part because it is unattainable and aims to enforce through delimitation an "illusion of autonomy."[75] Such an illusory autonomy, which would deny the fundamental connectivity of the I with not-I, results in an inertia and alienation as this supposedly unified I aims to endlessly adapt itself to the other and they-self that is the not-I.

The formations of the I are confronted with demands for unification and delimitation, whilst simultaneously they are unable to maintain this unification due to the very nature of their formation. And yet, as the mirror stage affirms, the self forms through interactions with that which is perspectivally transformed to become not-self. It returns again to the bottomless depths which are both of self and of beyond, to the realisation that "[i]n the self's own depths there must be the fact of the Self's own self-negation as constitutive of itself." [76] This formation of a sense of self in relation to that which is not self cannot be said to be telic, that is it cannot be characterised by a beginning and an end, by a point of initiation whereby this unfolding begins and dissolves the self, and a point of completion where the self becomes isolated and enclosed. Rather it is distributed throughout the self and is one of the conditions of its existence, it is a basic structure of being-there and of subjectivity, not a phase to be completed. It is a characterising of subjectivity as Dionysian, in a way that "subjectivity becomes a complete forgetting of the self." [77] In this way, subjectivity becomes inter-subjectivity, but an inter- that finds itself caught in a domain that cannot maintain the boundary between subject and object.

This continual undoing of the self that creates a continual interplay between the I and not-I leads to the existential self being a fleeting impossibility. Camus writes, "if I try to seize this self of which I feel sure, if I try to define and to summarize it, it is nothing but water slipping through my fingers… For ever I shall be a stranger to myself." [78] The self forever escapes articulation in the sense of a coherent whole, in the sense of a unified ego, in the sense of a contained life that is isolated and stands entirely opposed to death, that is to the entities that are beyond its perspectival limits. This self, this fleeting entity, is no sooner formed than once more it dissolves, no sooner born that it dies, and its endless births and deaths give it the character of an ungraspable liquid, an ever-transforming multiple becoming. A birth of self is accompanied by a death that sees it transformed to a not-self, and a death of self brings with it a birth of an alter-self, another not-self from the position of the other self that dies but remains present in its absence, that continues to exist not only in a line-arised past, but in a temporality that exceeds present and past and compels futures.

Throughout Proust's *Search* the self dies and is born. It is not only a dual split between the narrator's "social self" and the self that is the author as in the closing pages. But there is a continual proliferation of selves, a literary *ecology of selves*.[79] Even within the literary form of *The Search* there is a multiplicity of selves that cannot be reduced to each other, and that communicate endlessly — we are never sure where Proust ends and *The Search* begins, where the author and the narrator converge. But not only this, the narrator and the writer continually transform one another, producing a proliferation of perspectives that are themselves caught in the transformative power of involuntary memory. Where can we really say that *The Search* begins? Is it in Combray? Is it with the story of Swann that precedes the birth of both author and narrator? Or is it at the point of *Time Regained* where the narrator, after his long journey, becomes apparently united with the writer, where involuntary memory and the passage through its transformed past reaches a bottleneck and converges with the act of writing?

In the opening of *Time Regained*[80] the narrator of *The Search* finds that the paths upon which he trod in the past no longer hold the same wonder and amazement, and that the woman with whom he treads them, having once been the centre of his affections, no longer even appears to him as beautiful. The duration through which he has travelled has seen him so transformed that the perspective of his apparent former self now appears as alien to him. The vision of his youth, the beauty, wonder and excitement it perceived, has fallen through his hands; no longer do the places resonate as they once did, no longer does beauty appear as it once did. This death of the self is re-enacted countlessly, but it always brings with it birth. Death and life are unified in a becoming that is multiplicity itself and a multiplicity that is becoming itself.

There is a moment in *Sodom and Gomorrah* where the narrator of *The Search* is compelled, by a request from Swann, to take up his pen and write to Gilberte.[81] The narrator begins to write the name of this woman whom, in his youth, he loved and finds that the feeling of excitement, of trepidation, is no longer present. He now loves another, and his durative passage has transformed him. But it is not just a transformation along a linear temporality. There is a sudden proliferation of selves in communication—the self of a past love, the self of the apparent present, the multiple selves of Habit. There is a proliferation of pronouns—he, she, I— all relating to the same apparently discrete individuality that is the author of the name, and perhaps also the author of the words we read. "I" begins writing the name *Gilberte*, but realises that Habit ("she") has delegated the task to "one of the many secretaries whom she employs." This secretary, now a "he," can write the name *Gilberte* "without attaching any reality to the words" knowing only that it is a woman that "I" once loved for "he" has heard "I" speak of her. What can we make of this proliferation of selves? This clamorous ecology of pronouns?

The "I" that once loved Gilberte is not the same "I" that now is compelled to write to her. The "I" that trembled with excitement at writing the name has departed, it is dead; but that does not mean it is no longer active or present. It returns. This I that loved Gilberte returns and involuntarily reminds the I that writes her name of the past love, of the excitement that once existed when writing her name—it remains effective in apparent death. It emerges as the multiple "she" of Habit and its delegated "he," the inscription of a trace that now operates in a temporality that is beyond, not in the sense of a past comprised of moments that have passed, but a past that enters into the space of the always-already, of the formation of trace and habit, of the communication of dead selves with living selves that is the very contradiction of the self. It is not a question of the one discreet individual simply transforming but remaining continuous and self-same, but of a proliferation of individuals entering into tiny births and deaths. All these selves live and die continuously—it is a matter of intensities, rather than static states of vitality. The self that loves Gilberte communicates with the self that does not, and the selves of Habit enter into this communication. There is a proliferation of durations in connection, and expansion and interaction of durative-souls.

There are many deaths of the self within Proust. The narrator and the author endlessly recount the selves of the past that, whilst they have died, remain effective and in action, for they have always already been selves. So many things appear disenchanted that were once wondrous, as so many lives, thoughts and feelings are thrown into new light by the communication of multiple selves—words change content, music transforms, literary idols are made profane. There is not one self of *The Search*, but an opening, a self-ing that leaves the narrator, author and reader uncertain as to who is occupying which perspective and when. It is a locus of contradiction that undoes the inside of selfhood and opens it up to conjunctions and proliferations that are inescapably creative.

But the selves do not only proliferate in relations between other selves, in the sense of subjects, of other Is, shes or hes. The opening up of subjectivity by objectivity is also continually attested to. The famous madeleine, the twin steeples of Martinville, the uneven paving stones of the Guermantes courtyard, the hawthorn flowers, the music of Vinteuil, all of these factors impel the self outside of itself, and compel *The Search*. It is when faced with the world of things that memory comes forth so powerfully that it overwhelms the present moment. The hawthorn flowers, the uneven stones, the madeleine, are not called forth by the narrator, they are not objects given up to his thought and memory, he does not think through them; rather they think through the narrator — they move the narrator violently and forcefully. The world of dead things dissolves the inside of the living narrator, they bring him closer to death and themselves closer to life and in so doing, both enter into increased vitality.

So what then is this self that we are left with? It no longer can appear as an enclosed life, a delimited individuality. It is shown to continually open onto domains that are other than it in such a way that forbids its closure. What we are left with is an entity continually leaning towards multiplicity and so too becoming, and the self here emerges as "only a threshold, a door, a becoming between two multiplicities"[82] or more. It is this threshold, which as threshold, creates a locus of absolute contradiction as multiplicities pull from all directions, as connections and undoings proliferate, as the living and the dead intertwine and communicate.

Growth and Decay

The self then has been shown to constantly open up onto that which is not self, the I emerges from its opening unto the not-I. That bottomless space of absolute contradiction which contracts to create a discrete sense of individuality and closure continually unfolds to reveal its openings. So what then is the place of the individual? Has it not been dissolved amidst a domain of extensive communication in which life and death become one? Have not confusion and paradox won out, and has not a new nihilism that would deny the sovereignty of the individual emerged? Have we not created one of those earthly utopias that the scheme of telluric death enacted as its beyond? Has not an abstract Life, beyond any individual entity, emerged that would efface the durative singularity of the living and the dead?

The effacement of the individual under the banner of collectivity is an often enacted movement. The denial of the reality of individuality and the accompanying affirmation of the collective is key in the schemes of the beyond of telluric-death. The earthly utopias—Progress, Art, Race, Nation, Spirit, Communism and Capital—regularly appear as dominant abstractions which subordinate all-things under their banner, and dissolve the individual amidst webs of connectivity that, in being beyond the individual, are granted a greater degree of reality than it. Has not the dissolution of the self through the confronting of its own bottomless depths enacted such an effacement that would deny reality to the I-sayer?

These questions, in many respects, concern the very ground of the tendential connectivity of the living and the dead. They concern the passage of one apparently bound entity to that nothingness that is not *nihil* but the beyond of an inside, an *infinitum*. They concern the relationship of an entity to that which it is not, the relationship of the living and the dead. There also remains in these questions what could be seen as a confusion between that death which is the death-of-the-living, which would be an individualised-death, and the lifelessness-of-the-nonliving. Have we not made unclear the simple separation between the lifelessness-of-the-nonliving and the death and dying of life?

Which of these questions comes first? Is it a matter of logical precedence? Do we first ask of the relationship of individuality to connectivity, or do we ask of the relation between the individualised-death of the living and the lifelessness-of-the-nonliving? In many respects these questions are, if not the same, embedded in one another—what we interrogate is the relationship between a defined and delimited interior to that which lies beyond it, the permeability of the boundary and the passage across, between and through it.

So, it appears we cannot attribute a precedence of one question over the other—we must start from the middle. To ask one of these questions prior to the other would not only attempt a logical, arborescent hierarchisation, but would also fail to fully apprehend the subject matter at hand—that is the unity of apparently opposing domains through connective communication, the undoing of that polarisation, the violent imposition of which oppresses the living and the dead. But the question is persistent— in this discussion, have we not confounded the death and dying of the living with the lifelessness-of-the-nonliving? Is not the entry into the domain of the dead that the dying of the living enacts of a different order to the lifelessness-of-the-nonliving?

It is clear that an individual manifestation of life does degrade and fall unto death. The animated body which we saw as being ensouled and thus permitted entry to the domain of life deteriorates, and at that point where its deterioration is such that it no longer manifests those characteristics which formulated the Aristotelean hierarchy of souls, it is determined to be dead. It no longer forms an element of the inside of life, which at the most basic level was of nourishment and growth, but has unfolded to its exterior. Let us take this question of nourishment and growth briefly. In doing so, it is hoped that the relationship between the death-of-the-living and the lifelessness-of-the-nonliving may become clearer, and may be shown to be not entirely separate.

The most basic level of life, within the Aristotelean soulful stratification, was that of growth and nourishment and these characteristics of life were said to be found in the form of vegetative life and the forms of life hierarchised above it. At the most basic level, life grows and draws nourishment. The plant that grows does so by drawing upon its milieu—the soil, the sun, the water, the air, are all nonliving components of life, they are the death that allows for the unfolding of the living. The plant draws upon these dead elements, contracting them within an individual system that we recognise as living organised matter.

But this growth implies decay. "Life is always a product of the decomposition of life."[83] The living entity grows, but always within limits that are emergent to its situatedness as well as immanent to growth itself. Immanent as the foundations of nourishment which make growth possible — the dead soil, the decaying corpse, the fire, water, earth and air — and immanent as the threshold and boundary of growth's possibility, whilst still emergent of the situatedness of a milieu and contraction. The decayed ground of growth is both its possibility and limit, and in this sense it is both emergent from growth and immanent to it. It is the space of death that both gives the possibility of life and constrains it. The entity that grows draws from decayed dead matter, and death gives way to life. But the entity that grows also reaches limits and decays itself — entering into this domain of dead things that forms the basis of growth. The soil, minerals, air and water contract within the living entity until they unfold from the space of life and re-enter the domain of death.

The limit of growth is decay, but decay is also its possibility. Death and decay are a no-matter-what[84] in relation to life, both in the sense of a levelled playing field, but also the inevitability of their recurrence. The question of biological immortality may be thought of as an interruption to this — it may be said that there do exist living entities that escape the decaying of life — the lobster, hydra or immortal jellyfish. But it is never an absolute escape just as it is never an absolute severance, a finalist-death — the limits emerge in other ways and the nourished becomes nourishment and feeder becomes food elsewise. Predation, — the communication of predator–prey that too is a communication of the living and the dead — disease, exhaustion and injury enact a shortened decay, a contracted limit to growth. The lobster that grows endlessly collapses under its own growth, and the jellyfish that is threatened reverses its growth, short-cutting its flight unto death through a transdifferation that constitutes degrowth as a mode of alter-decay.

So, what is the individual entity that grows, is nourished and decays? What is an individual if it is born from death and returns to death, if it is formed and returns to that which it is not? It is, as with the living and the dead, a question of tendencies. There is a tendency of the individual to close itself off from its milieu, to become as self-sufficient as possible, to fold its situatedness inside itself for its own strength and survival—but this tendency is only ever partial. The same body that closes itself off from its environment must, in order to ensure its continuation, through nourishment and reproduction for instance, open itself unto that which it is not and from which it seeks severance.

There is an apparent perspectival split here that we cannot ignore. There is one sense in which death concerns individualities—the dying and death of an entity. Beyond this individualised-death the entity concerned is said to have died and no longer partakes in the interiority of life. It is this death that is expressed in existentialism in its Kierkegaardian form as a mode of judgment and the end of the sickness, and in the Heideggerian form as the ownmost potentiality of a being—they present a form of closure, a finality, a sealing and completing of an individual's potentiality: its authenticity or salvation. We do not entirely deny this perspective of the closure of a sense of self, of an I-sayer and a noetic experiential duration, and nor could we. But there is another perspective, a perspective of a form of superlative Life,[85] which would say that Life and Death do not belong to individuals who are just carriers and expressions of a current that exceeds them and of which they are just temporary manifestations. There are many manifestations of this latter perspective — Bergson's *élan vital*, Aristotle's *psukhē* or soul as the principle of life.

We will not attempt any kind of taxonomy or typology of these models of superlative Life, but instead focus upon that which is closest to what has been named the tendencies of life and death. In fact, the point of view of the tendential relationship of life and death does not necessarily oppose the notion of a superlative life or death—that is a life and death beyond the individualised living and dead, and the existential individualised-death. Rather, it concerns the reality and validity of both; their connectivity and unity.

Individuality

So what then is the individual if it is endlessly found to be opening onto that which it is not, in a way that undoes the boundaries of its delimitation? The individual life appears to be diminished in the face of a superlative Life, a Life that begins to look as though it might become a moral determiner. Have we arrived at a point where the individual is but "one beat in the pendulum of life,"[86] or "merely a bud that has sprouted on the combined body of both its parents?"[87] Such assertions would represent the perspective that would state that life does not belong to individuals, that is but a current passing through them that always exceeds them. Here life and death do not belong to the individual. They are currents that flow beyond any one body. They are tendencies that cannot adequately be thought when constrained to the life and death of individuals, for they do not belong to individuals and are not their properties. The life and death of an individual is nothing but a gradated locus of transition, and indeed one that is never absolute, one that is never final, one that is always tendential and partial.

Just as we cannot deny the reality of the existential confronting of death alone, of the ownmost standing before life and death in the situatedness of one's thrownness, so too we cannot deny the reality of life as that which exceeds an individual. Both hold reality. It is a matter of perspectival transformation and interpretation: not a relativistic isolation that would, at its extremity, deny the possibility of communication between incommensurable perspectives, but a perspectivism that remains continuous and connective. This is a perspectivism that rather than denying communication between isolated worlds, is one of situatedness,[88] of the inability to see beyond a horizon from any given position within an extensive network. As such, the existential confrontation of death in solitude is not in opposition to the life and death that exceed the individual in all directions — they belong to the extensive networks of becoming, but occupy different and varying perspectival positions. Just as the individual is a temporary locus of intensive materiality within a current that exceeds it, so too does the phenomenological experience of standing before one's life and death in solitude belong to a domain that is not isolated, but extensive and communicative.

It will be recalled that the self, upon turning on itself, dissolved amidst its own bottomless depths. This revealed that "each existential center radiates to infinity"[89] and that the very conditions of its formation as finite ensured openings to the infinite. It is this opening that ties eternity closely to all-things in connective communication and the confronting and recognising of this that was read in the *adequate ideas* of Spinoza's *Short Treatise*. It is this opening and radiation that when confronted allows us to grasp the tendential connectivity of the living and the dead as unity and possibility, and which implies the more it is recognised, as Spinoza oddly put it, "the less death is harmful to us."[90] And what is more, it is this opening radiation and connective communication that emerges as the thrownness of being-there and being-together-with. The existential-death is rooted in an opening that compels it beyond individualisation, beyond the ownmost and into a *they* that is no longer pejorative, lost or irresolute but infinite, extensive and connective. As such, the existential death and life, which may so often appear individualised, is individualised only as a tendency with that by which it is lost in the infinite depths of its own formation and being-there.

In both the processes of growth and decay, and the existential experiences of selfhood, the space of life, of the living entity, confronts that which it is not as the very basis of its formation. The

77

living entity draws upon spaces of death in order to live—growth draws upon decay, self unfolds to other, subject becomes object. There are tendencies that operate between these domains and processes of growth–decay, self–other, subject–object to such an extent that the tendency does not fluctuate between two opposing terms, but rather is itself the unity of these terms. The individual, then, stands before, is formed by and entangled with that which it is not. But this is not an entanglement of two closed systems that face one another, of a subject that confronts an object, of a self that confronts other, a growth that confronts decay, a life that confronts death. This is an entanglement that concerns the very basis of the formation of these apparently opposing entities, that locus of absolute contradiction that sees every finite entity radiating to infinity.

The living being confronts the world, and so too death, not as isolated and distinct from it, or as a closed and bound entity, but as continuous with the multiplicity in which it is immersed. As Deleuze and Guattari write on Bergson,

> If the living being resembles the world, this is true, on the
> contrary, insofar as it opens itself to the opening of the world; if it
> is a whole, this is true to the extent that the whole, of the world as
> of the living being, is always in the process of becoming, develop-
> ing, coming into being or advancing, and inscribing itself within a
> temporal dimension that is irreducible and nonclosed.[91]

The beyond of the living being is the beyond of a continual communication of a temporal dimension that exceeds it and remains open and extensive.

This lack of closure and extensive communication is not only found in the existential experience of the self confronting its own bottomless depths. The problem of biological individuality parallels the impossibility of clearly defining the boundaries of the I.

It is again a matter of perspectival transformation, of the molar judgment that would delimit and define the bound individuality and the molecular unfolding of that individuality at the infinitesimal level. The questions within biology of the boundaries of the individual organism reiterate this continuity that underpins the formation of self through other.

The forager who walks through the forest seeking mushrooms as a source of nourishment finds what they believe to be an individual being. The single cap is picked and a relationship of prey–predation/food–fed is enacted between what might appear as two individualities. But sustained reflection upon the *Armillaria bulbosa* reveals the complexity of defining its individuality. From our position as foragers we see this necrotrophic fungus as a series of discreet individualities, but below the surface of the earth the extensive network of rhizomorphs that connects the individual fruit bodies sees a genetically identical network extending across fifteen hectares for 1,500 years.[92] Is this vast entity that spreads across such expansive space and time an individual life, an organism, or is it an infection centre[93] of necrotrophy, of life coming forth from death?

The siphonophores again reveal this opening of individuality. Their colonial organisation that sees each specialised zooid communicating to form a complex emergent whole reveals the difficulty of where to ascribe individuality. Do we define the assemblage as an individual, or is it each zooid? The structures of the zooids are found elsewhere living as independent entities with their own individualised-life and -death, and yet in the assemblage of the siphonophore they live and die as a whole—in terms of evolutionary theory the zooid becomes the object of natural selection, and yet in terms of ecology it is the assemblage that functions as an individual. Where do we enact the count-as-one?[94] The assemblage of the siphonophores again reveals that life, not only humanity, is "not composed of isolated beings but of communication between them."[95] And to turn back upon ourselves from such a perspective, what would we find? The unity and organisation of organs in the form of an organism no longer seems so clear, no longer seems so obvious. We find that "every animal is fundamentally a band, a pack... We do not become animal without a fascination for the pack, for multiplicity. A fascination for the outside? Or is the multiplicity that fascinates us already related to a multiplicity dwelling within us?"[96] It is not only for the existential self that the coherence of an interiority is an impossibility, but for the tendency of life and death itself.

And again, Hermatypic coral reefs reveal this complexity and opening of individuality. Such corals are comprised of two parts: calcite deposits and polyps that grow and depend on the calcite.[97] The living component of the coral is comprised of a layer of polyps functioning as a cooperative colony. These polyps grow upon calcium carbonate, the nonliving foundation of the coral. In addition, the polyps secrete the calcite meaning that as the individual polyps come and go there is a continual collation of layers of calcium carbonate which form the reef. The combination of the calcite corallite and the polyp together form a modular zooid. It is the proliferation of these zooids by extension or multiplication that constitutes the growth of a coral reef—the coral reef grows only when living and nonliving are both able to flourish, only when life and death emerge in unity.

These brief examples reveal the same shattering of identity and coherence that the existential self confronts in approaching its own bottomless depths. It reveals that "every material entity is not really one entity. It is an essential multiplicity of entities."[98] It is not the isolation of the subject, the self, or of an all-too-human form of individualised and isolated consciousness alone that reveals a tendential relationship between an identity and that which it is not, but it is central to the very entanglement of becoming. The living entity opens up unto the world, and so too unto death, and the dead spaces in which it finds itself entangled —the necrotrophic ground of the fungus, the calcite, the non-self —are continuous with it. Such spaces are sources of nourishment and growth and so too decay; they are the foundational entanglements of the living and the dead. The organism is not one, but many, a constantly refolding and unfolding multiplicity of life and death.

Nature and Continuity

Take the arctic midge out of its frozen environment, remove this living, individual entity from the processes of freezing, and it will be unable to survive. This adaptation to environment that living entities possess reveals the inseparability of that entity deemed to be living from the domain of death with which it is continuous—the dead space of ice is the ground of the life of the arctic midge, it cannot live without it and so its life is born and sustained by a space of nonlife. Biologically this is explained in the notion of evolutionary adaptation, but at the basis of this notion rests a stubborn connectivity of the delimited entity with that which it is not, of the connectivity of its life with the nonliving spaces that surround it.

In the *Three Ecologies*, Felix Guattari illustrates the continuity of the supposedly separate domains of the human world of "culture" and the "natural" world through an experiment conducted by Alain Bombard:

He produced two glass tanks, one filled with polluted water - of the sort that one might draw from the port of Marseille - containing a healthy, thriving, almost dancing octopus. The other tank contained pure, unpolluted seawater. Bombard caught the octopus and immersed it in the 'normal' water; after a few seconds the animal curled up, sank to the bottom and died.[99]

The octopus cannot be separated from its environment for it cannot be said to stand outside of it. The sudden removal of the octopus from its dwelling place results in its death, its exposure to what is pharmacologically poisonous to its becoming. In this way, what appears as a delimited organism unfolds as entirely continuous with its environment. The environment is no longer the out-there, but permeates the organism, and can no longer stand beyond and outside it as death can no longer stand outside life.

If the organism is continuous with its environment then the line between the two dissolves alongside the line between the supposedly discontinuous domains of nature and culture, in a parallel manner to the undoing of the self, bio-individuality and the shattering of the subject. The question of "what adapts to what" loses its clarity—does the organism adapt to its environment, or can we say that the environment adapts the organism, or that the environment adapts to the organism? It is clear that organisms adapt environments in the way they modify flows of energy and also in the structures they create: the beaver's dams, spider's webs, urbanism. But also the entire environment can adapt to an organism—this has been highlighted through the increasing study of trophic cascades and the realisation that the reintroduction of predators to given ecosystems can so radically alter those ecosystems as to cause the rivers to change their course.

But then do we just extend the boundary, even as a boundary in process, and say that structures "external" to the organism are additional organs, are an "external physiology"[100]? Or would it not be better to allow the organism-environment to dissolve in continuity, to instead reveal a vast body without organs, an extensive ground of communication, connection and potential, a domain of conflict and continual imbalance that would be less nature than *phusis*? Would it not be better to do away with the interaction and adaptation that insistently bifurcates, and instead confront the tendential and processual unity of opposing entities? Would we not return to Heraclitus[101] and come to see the split between individual and environment, subject and object, as a matter of perspectival transformation, and would not the process-based characteristics of this continuity that is only shattered by perspectival interpretation reaffirm that "becoming and multiplicity are the same thing"?[102]

What this shows is the insistent continuity of the domain that has been labelled and restricted as nature—that its splitting up into subjects and objects, organisms and environments, individuals and species, attempts but never fully achieves a concealment of the continuity of communication. Such continuity leads us back to a nature that is not *res extensa*, that is not somehow "out there" or on the outside, but is continuous and connective. And here we return to *phusis* not simply translated as nature and seen through the all-too-human lenses of anthropomorphism, but rather as that primordial gathering and conflict, a *phusis* prior to restriction and discontinuity,[103] a conflict between elements that are always coming-together, gathering.

So we have begun to see the dissolution of the veil of Mâya that would separate the active, knowing and fruitful subject from the world of mere objects; it disintegrates as self opens up onto other, subject onto object, growth onto decay and individuals onto non-closures. The domain of the outside of life now appears as no longer outside. It is not that the inside has been brought outside or the outside in; it is a case of the diffusion of both. The domain of "nature," which would once have appeared as split apart by the subject/object distinction that makes of matter a substratum for sense-perception, now appears as something radically different. No longer can it be posited as that which is "out there" and given up to the sensibility of the living. Rather the living and dead, the organism and its environment, stand forth together in the continuity and conflict of *phusis*.

Contemplation and Forgetting

So what does this continuous domain of conflict, continuity, rupture and gathering do, if not think and contemplate? How can it only be the subject and the interior of life, and further the highest pinnacle of the interior of life, that is permitted to enter into the privileged domain of reflection, action and thought? What is an entity, if not a contemplation of the elements of which it is comprised, of its contraction and the interactive contemplation of the conditions of its formation? As Deleuze writes,

> What we call wheat is a contraction of the earth and humidity, and this contraction is both contemplation and the auto-satisfaction of that contemplation. By its existence alone, the lily of the field sings the glory of the heavens, the goddesses and gods — in other words, the elements that it contemplates in contracting. What organism is not made of elements and cases of repetition, of contemplated and contracted water, nitrogen, carbon, chlorides and sulphates, thereby intertwining all the habits of which it is composed? [104]

Here is the tendency of life and death that in contemplative becoming emerges in the wonder of goddesses and mortals. The humidity and soil, the nitrogen and carbon, the chlorides and sulphates, live not, or so the inside of life declares, and yet their folding, contracting and auto-satisfaction brings forth that which is recognised as living, that which is permitted, albeit in this case at the lowest of the stratified levels, to enter into the domain of life. The dead bring life in contemplation and birth, and death returns the living to the grounds of their emergence — there is no clear line, no inside–outside that could separate them, but only foldings of contemplations, the undoing and unbecoming of beings, and their continual unfolding into that nothingness that is not *nihil*, but quite simply the limit of their being. [105]

Undoubtedly, biology draws the line of the living and the nonliving — but two entities delimited under the same conditions by biology — two seeds, two grains of wheat — will emerge and flourish differently under different skies, on different soils, surrounded by different lives and deaths. Those apparently dead elements — the sulphates and the chlorides — fold together and contemplate one another, as they contemplate the direction of the wind and the fall of the rain, as they contemplate the sunlight above and the soil below, and in their contemplating form a vitality that comes to be recognised as living. That which is dead draws out life and life too draws out death.

This contemplation is not of a divine nature, it does not return to the One or the transcendental plane of forms, it is not gifted to the wheat or the sulphates by an all-encompassing force of pure thought, but is immanent to them, to the chlorides and the carbon, the rain and the sun, the seed and the soil. They contemplate one another in the being of a between that affirms becoming as the being of Being. The soil contemplates the seed and the seed the soil. This is not a mysticism, but a communication, a communication that is not limited to the realm of the living precisely because it is of communication. Growth, decay and nourishment, those elements of the basest Aristotelean soul, are not the exclusive domain of an inside of life, but are elements of a contemplation that defies the formation of such an inside, that does not lead up to the Word or the One, but remains immanent to those entities which contemplate and are contemplated simultaneously, on the same level.

Such contemplation offends the sensibilities of the interior of life and the elevated position granted to Man amongst things. Life is the active interior, and the dead may not contemplate life for only the subject contemplates. But the active nature of the interiority of subjective life is continually undone. The activity of remembering, of the bringing-forth of memory, shows us this.

Throughout Proust this undoing of the active nature of interior subjectivity is continually enacted. The continual failure of voluntary memory defies the active interior of the subject—it is not the subject that remembers for itself. At the moment when *Lost Time* becomes *Time Regained* in the final chapter of *The Search*,[106] the contemplation of the narrator by the past is attested to. It is not the narrator of *The Search* that contemplates his past, but the past that contemplates him. And it is this contemplation of Proust's narrator that creates a regained time, a time that radically transforms the preceding pages, and casts them in an entirely new light, that reveals memory orientated not towards the past but towards the future. The narrator does not reflect actively on an inactive past, he does not call forth his memory in order to reflect upon it; the memory—not entirely in truth belonging to him—calls him forth with such force and violence that he is transformed and the entirety of *The Search* is redefined and reinterpreted. It is the past that contemplates Proust, not Proust who contemplates his past.

But with this contemplation also comes forgetting, and it is with forgetting that thought becomes thought as such. Borges[107] and Kohn[108] describe how thought, and the ability to think, are characterised less by remembering than by forgetting. "Thinking is forgetting differences,"[109] Borges writes, for if that which thinks only remembered it would simply be an accumulation of everything, of all impressions, engagements and contemplations —there would be no discernment or separation, no distinguishing or identification. The numerous tiny deaths and births through which any given durative-soul passes must be inscribed, but also in their inscription is their selection, the discarding of that which it no longer is, that which has died, and that which has been born as its replacement. This is the memory of the durative-soul, a memory of forgetting more than it is remembering, for as Klossowski asks, "*How can memory subsist* if it has to deal with things that no longer belong to the self? *How can we remember as a being that can remember everything except itself?*"[110] That which thinks has to forget in order to know, in order to enact that violence that is the delimitation and separation from continuity of an object of knowledge — to traverse the passage from misosophy to philosophy. That which thinks, not in the sense of the marked interiority of the subject but in the sense of the entities that know through forgetting, engages in tiny deaths that birth knowledge; forgettings that give life.

This knowledge is not only a subjective affect or discursive formation, but it also emerges as an entity that could be labelled objective — this is how evolution produces the organism, through a forgetting of forms that produces the species as it is through a forgetting that produces specialisation and adaptation to environment and world. Evolution thinks and knows as the environment thinks and knows through these forgettings and these tiny deaths of emergent forms. It is the forgetting of the failures of the past bodies of a species that lead to its emergence having been moulded by the absence of the past. This is the presence through absence of the past in the present and the pressing of a present absence on the future. Thus the eternal return is as much a forgetting as it is a recurrence—it is a return of difference that in being different is the forgetting and tiny death of the same. The emergence of difference, the use of history for life and vitality, comes from the death of the remembered—its forgetting. In this way death moulds life as the forgetting which produces the different as well as knowledge and the delimited form.

CHAPTER 3

Beyond Life

Sex, Shit, Beasts and Powerful Communication

We have seen how the disillusion of the interiority of life — that is, the violent call of death that demands the continual unfolding of the living into the spaces of the nonliving, the many births and deaths that any durative-soul endures and that cause its swelling — was not only found at a phenomenological or existential level, but unfolds continually also in the domain of *phusis*. The problem of bio-individuality revealed a parallel to the problem of the existential self. From both perspectives, the demand that the continuous tendencies of life and death should be aggressively and statically bifurcated into discontinuous states of Being was denied, and the ability of maintaining such boundaries was brought into question. So too do we find in the moral orders and boundaries of taboo and transgression an interplay between supposedly separated domains, by which the unfolding of life into death is revealed and so too the unfolding of the dead into the living.

The taboo and the transgression are equiprimordial. That is to say that the establishment of a taboo is also the act of a transgression. No barrier would need to be erected were the transgressive behaviour not assured to occur. As such, the erection of barriers and discontinuities that the moral order of taboo installs enacts a splitting up of the continuous whilst also dismantling and dissolving these boundaries. Integral to the forbidding that the taboo instigates, is an acknowledgement of the impossibility of the absolute banishment of transgression. Within the apparently absolute system of morality and the banishment of certain acts, thoughts and feelings, is an implicit, if sometimes unacknowledged, awareness that this banishment cannot be maintained, that the splitting up of the continuous can never be absolute. The creation of the interiority of the moral order carries with it the inevitability of its disillusion.

It is not by accident that what is found in so many taboos is the attempted banishment and minimisation of the continuous, the attempted partitioning off of life, and its highest pinnacle, from the world which it inhabits and with which it cannot be anything other than continuous. Such taboos include those associated with sexuality, defecation, animality, cannibalism, obscenity and death. All of these forbidden domains reveal to life its inseparability from the flux and flow of becoming; they deny the hyperbolic naïveté and arrogance of Man, for what they present us with is the inescapability of eternal connection and extensive duration.

In the sexual act, two supposedly distinct beings are unified and dissolve amidst one another. This disillusion is not only a phenomenological or experiential process, but is a material and physical one. Nevertheless what is revealed in the phenomenological experience of sexual union is the profound and in fact violent dissolution of discontinuity, the inescapable call of another that compels the I-sayer beyond themselves and thus beyond life. The call of another in the sexual act comes as much from the supposed self as it does from the other, "in the intensity of pain or pleasure, and especially in voluptuousness, the 'person' disappears for a moment."[111] In this respect, the sexual act reveals the Sublime as that moment when the doctrine of individuality and the faculties can no longer maintain itself, at that moment when the supposedly discontinuous faculties swell, overload and overspill leading to their discordancy, disarmament and disillusion, "[i]t is a tempest in the depths of a chasm opened up in the subject."[112] In the sexual union, two entities do not simply enter into some kind of synthesis, but overspill their delimitation and dissolve amidst powerful communication.

This *powerful communication*[113] is central to the dissolution of discontinuity and interiority that compels supposedly separated beings beyond the boundaries of their delimitation. This is not a communication between two distinct and delimited beings, but is the persistent insistence of experience, consciousness and subjectivity within the space of another, the compulsion of interiority to go beyond itself, to find its possibility beyond itself, and the profound intimacy this produces. It is a scandal of consciousness, "[t]he scandal is the *instantaneous* fact that consciousness is consciousness of another consciousness, that is, the look of another look."[114] It is the moments of dissolution, moments when discontinuity can no longer be maintained, when rationalised works of partitioned entities dismantle, that call forth a powerful communication that compels entities beyond themselves — these are the moments of love, sexuality, carnivalesque celebration, death, birth.

Such a mode of communication far exceeds the linguistic or the symbolic, and reveals the place of semiotics and language as only one, and in fact an incredibly small, domain of experience and possible communication. And what powerful communication reveals is in one sense the nonlinguistic, nonsemiotic foundation of language, the space of poetic communication that always exceed the functionalised and rationalised functions of the linguistic domain. This is how the famous deconstructivist statement "*there is nothing outside of the text* [there is no outside-text; *il n'y a pas de hors-texte*]"[115] is here to be understood — not that there is nothing other than text, not that the realm of discourse and intertextuality is everything, but that language, text and discourse are always entangled in becomings and connections that exceed language. If poetry is poetry it is because it makes use of language to dissolve language, and compels individualised-life into a space of death that reveals the continuity and connection of the supposedly discontinuous living and dead entities.

There is a sense then in which powerful communication is always a transgression of some law or other, that is some system of discontinuity and separation, some order of judgment, it is the continual recurrence of exceptionality as the very foundation of exception. In the transgression of taboo and moral order powerful communication emerges; as when standing before the corpse or entering mourning, in poetic expression the systematisation of language as a pragmatic conveyor of meaning is undone, and language is turned against function, against work, it is given over to Evil. So too does the transgression of the moral divides that separate Man from animality, person from person, and life from death bring forth modes of communication that overspill discontinuous entities and deny those very separations.

So what now then is the animal, stood in relation to the human? Can we still even consider entertaining the kind of arrogance that allowed us to demean and degrade the animalistic entity to the position of an animal-machine, a merely reactive, mechanised being denied the same degree of life as Man? Can Kant's declaration that the animal is a mere thing which the human, being the pinnacle of life, can dispose of as they please, can do with as they please, be maintained any longer? If the unfolding of life unto death that has been revealed through the inescapability of connective continuity, and the nonliving and the dead have been brought into thought and the living through tendential interaction, must not the animal also be raised up alongside these now-liberated entities which we all become-with?

The humanistic outcry, the call of the *Gottmensch*, is one that would declare such a movement to be dehumanising and dangerous. It is a cry that would stand above all else and pass judgment whilst simultaneously raising itself up into the spaces of the transcendent divine. But we have seen that this is a perspective run through with hyperbolic naïveté and rampant arrogance, it is a position that demands a statified opposition of not only forms of life, but of life and death more generally, a statified opposition that grants the interior it delimits for itself absolute sovereignty over all-things, and ignores the call of powerful communication. It is this perspective—one that demands an elevated position for the form of life that is determined as Man—that enforces the hierarchical degradation of other entities, the divine substance of the soul resting atop a highly stratified organisation of Being and in turn being the only bringer of meaning and determiner of value. And as such, it is only this perspective that allows for the possibility of dehumanisation in the first place.

Latour has recently put this clearly when he writes,

> Far from being 'lowered down', 'objectified humans' will instead be elevated to the level of ants, chimps, chips, and particles! To be 'treated like things', as we understand it now, is not to be 'reduced' to mere matters of fact, but allowed to live a life as multifarious as that of matters of concern.[116]

The upsurge in what is referred to variously as object-oriented ontology and speculative realism among other names is significant. The current interpretation of this moment is perhaps one that many of the authors of these works would not themselves enact, or maybe even appreciate, but in the context of the current work, we can see in them a confronting of Man's hyperbolic naiveté and rampant arrogance, and acknowledgement of the connectivity of durative-souls and the belonging of such souls to entities well beyond the human and life. At the basis of what has become called the "ontological turn" we find a confrontation of the tendential connectivity of the living and the dead, their inseparability and continuity. There operates in these perspectives a flattening of the hierarchies of substance that placed the noetic soul at the pinnacle of life and demeaned all other entities to positions of lesser significance.

This leads us to a situation where Gabriel Tarde's considerations that all entities, not only the human, come together in ways that could be considered as social is reignited and reimagined.[117] In the context of human-animal relations this leads to a profound reconsideration of the hierarchy that placed the human at the pinnacle of life. Animals can no longer be considered lesser beings than the human; the Big Gaps that are endlessly functionalised in order to separate the human species from all other entities become recognised as continuous with chains of thought which exceed the bounded limits of the noetic soul. Eduardo Kohn has recently described such a consideration through the notion of the living thought.[118] Here, the consideration is that any entity that communicates through the use of signs should be considered as part of a continuous chain of thought, and the phenomenon of human thought and language is in fact only possible due to its continuity with this chain that far exceeds them.

Kohn's work draws specifically on the field of Peircean semiotics and the more recent field of biosemiotics. In this way his work becomes limited to the fields of communication between signs. For all the brilliance of this work and its undoing of the hyperbolic naïveté of Man this foundation in semiotics fails to approach the true profundity of modes of communication which exceed the domains of signs. If we recall the reinterpretation of the famous statement that there is no outside text as referring not to the universality of language, but to its entanglement in becomings and connections that always exceed it, that are always lost amidst *différance*, that meaning is born of a context that exceeds the domain of the linguistic, and appreciate its implications, we begin to see that thought, life and death are entangled in tendential connections that will always exceed the sign. The unfolding of life into death, the continual feedback and interplay between supposedly distinct domains, the connection and swelling of durative-souls, all reveal modes of communication that go beyond the exchange of signs and cannot be encapsulated by them.

We stand before this excess perhaps most clearly in those moments where the self entirely dissolves — in the heat of the sexual act, in the horror of confronting objects of fear, in the revelation of the sublime, in the agony of love, in the domain of eroticism. In such moments, a powerful communication unfolds that extends consciousness into an unconsciousness that is not an individualised domain of repressed thought and sensation, but an unconsciousness that quite simply reveals the fact that our connectivity and entanglement always exceeds the bounded limits of selfhood and individuality, that life always goes beyond the living, that we are part of a machinic phylum[119] that leads us to be continuous not only with other creatures and forms of life, but also with metals, chemicals and the entities that are so end-lessly marginalised to the ineffective, inactive spaces of nonlife and death. This is not only a powerful communication limited to the domain of inner experience, but a powerful communication of the association and mingling of bodies, a collision of bodies that at base undoes the barrier between the living and dead.

The continuity of life and death, their tendential, inescapa-ble and connective continuity, manifests through such modes of powerful communication. It is in such moments that we come face to face with our connective continuity with the living and the dead, and we find the very possibility of life is formed and forms the beyonds of life. But once again these are not beyonds of a transcendent divine or essential nature, they are beyonds that dissolve us amidst continuity and leave our efforts to grasp the self, to state I, to declare our absolute individuality, as desperate spasms, and stuttered and fleeting articulations. In so many of the spaces of transgression we confront entities that have been discarded and dismissed from the domains of the living, being assigned to the degraded and illegitimate domain of death.

Tools, Technics and Exteriorisation

There are various Nilotic narratives of creation that can be read as speaking to notions of division, telling of segmentations and stratifications of a once-unified continuity. According to one narrative[120] the earth was already created but due to prevalent darkness was indistinguishable from the sky. Divinity made mankind, and one named Aruu Pabek, but in the darkness Aruu could not see and so asked divinity for eyes; divinity refused, instead giving Aruu an axe. Aruu took the axe and hit the ground asking why it would not light up. From this blow to the ground one part rose above and another below and light shone across the Earth. Divinity asked of Aruu why he had done this for now he was a prisoner and could not return to the unity prior to the separation of earth and sky, divinity asked why Aruu had used the axe which was a gift to him for this purpose. From this point on death came into existence and any person who sought to return to the sky, to divinity, was killed. This division of earth and sky introduced both death and the need to labour; from that point on people had "to labour for the food they need."[121] This narrative is one of separation and division; this fundamental division is expressed in the Dinka phrase *piny aci bak* that literally translates to "the world has divided," but is used to signify dawn.

Such a focus on the unity of divinity can show how Nilotic cosmologies affirm fundamental ontological connectivities. Divinity, which grants sovereignty to the *reth* of the Shilluk, is characterised by connection and unity; the sovereign is of this unity rather than the embodiment of an everlasting spirit, thus it is not the kingship that is divine but connectivity, the unity of substance, form, causality and affect. The condition of humanity is one of separation from a lost unity, a prior total connectivity; through this separation both death and the need for labour are introduced. Technics, mortality and the world of work emerge alongside one another through stratifications of primordial connection. Aruu's use of the axe to separate the world is important for it introduces him to the objective world of practice and utility; Aruu, when he "makes use of the tool, becomes a tool himself, he becomes an object just as the tool is an object."[122] The use of the tool signals a removal of mankind from an instantaneity of existence and moves into a position of living and operating for the future, into a domain of anticipation that is aligned with the ever-approaching horizon of death. Aruu struck the ground in hope of a future answer to the question of why there is no light; he anticipated a response or effect of his action. Aruu enters a domain of anticipation, the anticipation of future utility, and the anticipation of death as inevitable but contingent possibility. Henceforth mankind labours for future gain, activity is considered in terms of future utility, and "the tool's meaning is given in the future, in what the tool will produce, in the future utilization of the product."[123] The use of the tool, and the introduction of labour, signals mankind's separation from divinity, the loss of sovereignty.

The loose parallels here with the more canonical tale of Prometheus' enchaining are clear. In both instances technics are granted to moral life, and in so receiving them they are condemned. Technics emerges alongside and through death, thanatology emerges with technology, and as in Nilotic cosmology, they stand forth together. "All human skill and science was Prometheus' gift."[124] The gift of fire from Prometheus, alongside the gift of the trace, grant the living engagement with the domain of the dead, that is with the domain of future anticipation in which technics emerges and develops, technics as a creative worlding that is focused on the future, which is, like death, anticipated continually by the living. The forever unfinished basis of life, its unfolding into technics, and the forever fleeting horizon of death which is equiprimordial with life and a condition of the possibility of its existence emerge alongside one another.

Technics then is revealed to us as a foray into the future, as an alignment with the temporal dimension of anticipation and projection. The tool should not only be considered as an object, it carries with it a whole logic of organisation and division that transforms dependent on the means of interpretation. With each tool is carried the implication of all technics, of a thanatic organology, a "theory of instruments"[125] and organisation of the nonliving through and alongside life. The *world of things* that was discussed in the preceding chapter is a manifestation of such logics of organisation—but as a manifestation and articulation in which the tendential connectivity of living and dead, of hand and hammer, of mind and tool, is reduced to a mechanised, function-ised and rational organology, a "standing reserve."[126] Here there is a system of organisation that would rationalise and function-alise even the living in the figure of a finalist, and thus fatalist, death; that is, a death devoid of its tendential connectivity with the living, the death that emerges as the image of closure and rupture. But the tool also articulates itself as an organ, that is as a component of a body that extends beyond the limits of the organism, it forms an extensive organology in which both those elements deemed to be living and those discarded as dead must be granted efficacy.

As with the case of Aruu Pabek, tools and technics become objects of anticipation; they orient us towards the future, and in so doing enter the domain of anticipation in which we experience our individualised-death as the final indeterminate anticipation, that possibility that is most certain. Both technics and death orient us towards the future, both share spaces of anticipation in which we continually unfold into a domain that is other than life, a domain of nonlife, a domain of death. Thus death and technics unfold as dually constraining and creative modes of anticipation, modes of orientation towards beyonds. This organology, this commons of the living and the dead, reveals not the mastery of the living over the dead, not the absolute efficacy of life and the inanimacy of the nonliving, but their codependence, and tendential connectivity, their becoming-with through the passage of tiny deaths and births and the continual unfolding and refolding of the living and the dead unto one another. Thus, the space of technics is not an outside of life, for as we have already seen maintaining this exteriority becomes absurd as the level of scale is altered. Rather the space of technics is continuous with the space of life, it is part of it, and as such the space of death that is the technical sphere is continually unfolding into the space of the organism — life cannot claim mastery over technics as though the space of technics were the space of mere matter, the substratum of substance that permits for the elevation of the all-too-human soul.

Thus, as Stiegler writes, "technics is the pursuit of life by means other than life."[127] The domain of the technical object is not outside of life, but forms an element of its very becoming and pursuit, its anticipation and evolution. To ignore the diffusion of life within technics — that is, the continual tendential interplay between life and death that constitutes the technical sphere itself — is to assign it to the domain of finalist-death, that domain of nonactive, ineffective merely dead things. This technicisation of *phusis*, where technics is refined to the ineffective and inactive mechanical being, leads to an enframing of all-things — that is, a mass disenchantment and mechanisation of an ineffective and external nature of finalistically dead beings; a standing-reserve. Thus it is not a case of becoming technophobic, of rejecting technics and so also becoming thanatophobic, but of confronting and re-enchanting our relationship to it. For seemingly paradoxically, when the technical sphere is assigned to the space of a mechanised finalist-death, to the place of a standing-reserve, far from becoming masters of it, we are enslaved unto it. Our persistent myopia is magnified, and we become blind to the action of the dead upon the living, that is of the refolding of the technical tendencies into the self and collectives of life. And in this way we unfold life also as mechanised and functionalised, that is under the domination of the monolithic universality of normative rationalisation.

Technics, then, cannot be a mere means, it must become understood not only as a mode of revealing if revealing is taken to mean an uncovering of what already exists in a cause, but rather it must unfold as an active creation, an extensive organology in which the domain of life and the domain of death are inseparable and in continual tendential connectivity, forming and shaping one another. We stand within the organology of technics, but the organology of technics also stands within us, as a condition of existence, as an ever-fleeting horizon of our eternal incompletion. Thus the being of technics is also that of unfolding, becoming and a creative revealing. *Phusis* stands forth as an originary conflict, no longer originary as an origin or original moment, but originary in the forever-incomplete process of creation. It is not only life that is unceasing creation,[128] but death too as the horizon to which life pursues and unfolds. And it is to the extent that "life is, more than anything else, a tendency to act on inert matter,"[129] that this apparently inert matter, from a mere inversion of perspective, enacts a tendency to act on the living to the extent that the unfolding of one unto the other through their tendential connectivity throws into absurdity the inertness of apparently dead matter. Technics is not the means, and neither is it an ends, but an unfolding of the primordial conflict in which life and death are co-constitutive and equiprimordial, in which life dances with and through death, and death with life.

What this tendential connectivity between the organology of the dead and the living — that is the system of organisation and theory of instruments that cuts across the division of life and death in a way that reveals each as inseparably caught and entangled in the other and continually unfolding unto the other — shows is that unfinished basis of life that sought the image of death as its closure. But we have seen that the unfinished basis of life does not meet death as its absolute closure, as its rupture, or even only as its ownmost potentiality, but that rather that domain of the dead is caught in this eternal incompletion, and by a manner in which its becoming and its multiplicity are but reverberations of the same sound heard from different perspectives. Becoming is never finished, the living unfold as entities which are never complete, revealing a process of exteriorisation[130] that has no outside and that unfolds being and our being as becoming, and becoming as the being of Being. The domain of death stands before us then as the indeterminate possibility of this unfolding, as the domain both of exteriorisation and the continual anticipation of this exteriorisation, as the unfolding of interiority unto exteriority in a way that the confounds the very exteriority to which it appears to unfold. The tool confronts us with our unfinished being, with our continual unfolding and dissolving, with our endless foray into, amongst and towards death.

Should we fail to approach technics beyond ends and means, beyond the calculation that demands of *phusis* that it become a standing-reserve and system of mechanisation, an instrumentalised organology of finalist-death and so too thanatophobia, we cannot help but become instrumentalised ourselves, and stand in relation to this instrumentalised conception of technics as subservient and fatalised, as instruments within a demeaned and degraded *world of things* devoid of sovereignty and powerful communication. The world becomes disenchanted, and the flight of the gods unfolds the nihilistic core of a mechanised universe. Not only Heidegger but also Nietzsche and Marx express this — we become dead-labour and instruments of the fatalism of capital, or nihilistic carriers of our own self-perpetuating voids. Our continuity with the world is shattered, and love, life and death are separated through the violent reverberations of this technicisation. It is this technicisation, which is a technics understood as instrumentalisation of means and ends and devoid of agency and efficacy, that operates within the *world of things* and the machinery of capital, within the domain of formalist economic reason of efficiency, scarcity and rationalisation. And it is this image of technics and technical organisation that is captured in the violent finalist-death-drive and so-called thanaticism[131] of contemporary economics, that is an understanding of the dead-thing as an entirely inactive, rationalised and mastered entity, as the dead-labour that stands in the service of the living and is granted no efficacy over the living.

As the speed of this space of a technics of finalist-death — of technics taken to be a mere standing-reserve — accelerates, increasingly approaching the terminal velocity that Marx warned of in the *Grundrisse*,[132] the manner in which we approach technics as being more than a rationalisation, instrumentalisation and system of means and ends becomes a question all the more severe and pertinent. The power of technics within the world of life cannot be approached if it is only interpreted through the scheme of finalist-death, that is through the constitution of a space that enacts the absolute exclusion of life from its domain. For what is at stake is an element of an endlessly ignored and marginalised "active relation of man to nature, the direct process of the production ... of the social relations of his life, and of the mental conceptions that flow from those relations."[133] It is an exclusion of the dead by the living that in turn enacts a domination of the living by the image of finalist-death, a death of mere mechanisation and inertness, a death of closure, rupture and the absolute negation of life, a death of a nihilistic void of less than nothing. Thus the approaching of technics cannot be separated from the disenchantment of mere matter that emerges through the hierarchisation of the all-too-human soul over the substratum of substance, to the extent that "[e]ven a history of religion that is written in abstraction from this material basis is uncritical."[134] For even the domains of the transcendent, of the durative-soul and its concealment through the hierarchisation of life that would place Man at its pinnacle, cannot be considered outside of the materiality of technics. And so too the instrumentalisation of a disenchanted *phusis* cannot be considered outside of this context, that of the tendential flow between life and death and the swelling and collision of durative-souls.

The technical object, the tool and the entire active domain of nonlife that reverberates throughout the living that it carries with it reveal the profound connectivity of life and death, the unfolding of life into death and death into life in a way that leaves both as objects of unfinished anticipation. And the relation between these two supposedly distinct and separate domains reveals to us:

> the fact that inert, although organized, matter qua the technical object itself evolves in its organization: it is therefore no longer merely inert matter, but neither is it living matter. It is organized inorganic matter that transforms itself in time as living matter transforms itself in it interaction with the milieu... matter organized technomorphologically is not passive... This technical phenomenon is the relation of the human to its milieu, and it is in this sense that it must be apprehended zoo-logically.[135]

Thus, the relation of the living standing before the unfinished image of itself in the sphere of technics must be apprehended as part of a machinic phylum[136] in which the bifurcated domains of life and death enter into tendential connectivity and exchange, each transforming and swelling one another and the singularity of the durative-souls which interact and collide.

In contrast, by focusing on technology as a dead, external object, a mere mechanical element, a calculable factor of a determined formula, we become blind to its wonder—that of the connectivity of the worlds of the living and dead, the folding of the dead into the spaces of the living and the continual unfolding of life into a space of death. Through technology the dead speak to the living daily, they call them forth, alter them, engage with them and compel them onwards, and daily the living unfold to the dead, transforming the domain of technology as a domain that stands outside of an individualised-life whilst being entirely entangled with life and death. And so "in our sheer preoccupation with technology we do not yet experience the coming to presence of technology"[137]; that coming to presence of technology is its standing before us as a site of total connection, as a site that violently dissolves our individualised being and forces us to an exteriorisation that is a tiny death in as much as it unfolds the interiority of life into a space that persists beyond the limits of individualised-life. And so technology unfolds in its eternal incompleteness as a mode of worlding, a creative force of construction, connection and communication rather than just a dead, static, instrumentalised domain of standing-reserves. And it is this creative worlding that engages the domains of poetics and powerful communication in a manner that not only undoes individuality and life, but also reveals the myopic limits of rationalised language.

Dwelling

Where does life dwell? And for that, where do we find death dwelling? Is it not apparent throughout the preceding discussions that life dwells in death and death dwells in life? The question then becomes a matter of how the living dwell in the dead, and how the dead dwell in the living, how they inhabit one another, how they transform one another, and how they provide spaces of cohabitation with one another. To say that life dwells in death and death in life is a matter of asserting their absolute inseparability and interdependency, their co-constitution and continual

engagement, their endless passage between one another revealing the supposedly discontinuous domains as continuous, as
reverberating throughout one another, as transformative intensities and consistent yet fluctuating vibrations. The tiny deaths
and tiny births through which all passages of becoming pass, and
through which they unfold bring forth an ecological domain, a
commons of life and death.

The hermit crab is perhaps one clear example of a living entity
that quite literally dwells in death. It is the death of the other
that provides the dwelling place of the hermit crab, here immediately understood quite simply as the material shelter but also as
the conditions of its possibility, the very foundations of its life.
This is not simply the death of the other that is a clearing of space
for the next form of life, although that is undoubtedly a part of
such a dwelling; rather it is a condition of the life of the hermit
crab itself, an immanent element of its becoming-with life and
death, what the older philosophy might have put down to being
a part of its "essence." The life and existence of the hermit crab
requires the death of other forms of life, it requires a space of
death that is not inactive and lacking in agency, a merely reactive death that would be the subordinate and degraded space of
a finalist and fatalist death that is naught but *nihil* and worse,
less than *nihil*, that is the closure and rupture of life. Rather it
requires a space of death that forms an element of its very life,
the possibility of its flourishing.

It is true that the hermit crab does not only dwell in the
directly discarded spaces of other forms of life, but where it does
not it nevertheless requires a space of nonlife as the foundation
of its possibility. And this space of nonlife reveals itself also as
an unfolding of the domain of the living into the domain of the
dead, a tiny death, a creation of an extensive entity and passage of
becoming that extends beyond the living and undoes its supposed
interiority, an unfolding of a living domain in extensive connec-

tion with that which will always be its beyond. This space of non-life is too a space of death, but spaces of death that are caught and entangled with the spaces of life to which they grant the possibility of their living. Life and death once again stand forth as inseparable, revealing themselves from the mist of discontinuity as connective and continuous, as unified opposites that only become opposites through forceful separation; the latter is not the negation or closure of the former, it is not degraded and consigned to the space of *nihil*-death or finalist-death, and life and death do not put themselves forward as absolute. In such a way they are in tendential becoming, a dance of co-flourishing in which the consideration of one without the other is but an absurdity.

Indeed the spaces of death that the hermit crab inhabits, that grant it the possibility of life, could even often be said to be spaces of death in relation to the forms of life from which they initially emerge, that is from the immediate perspective of those forms of life, not only their perspectival transformation by their engagement with the hermit crab. The snail's shell is an inescapable extension and part of its delimited living being, but it is a part of a living being that clearly and concisely reveals the tendential relationship of life and death, the dependent co-flourishing of the living and their endless and inescapable dances of becoming-with. The skeleton, the calcium foundation of marine polyps, the snake's shedable skin—these are all elements of delimited individualities and species-beings, but so too are they elements that remain and persist beyond the delimited individualised-life that we ascribe to the short life between an individuality's birth and degradation.

Let us think of another case of a living entity that dwells in the death of another individualised-life, not only in the very immediate sense of its material space of cohabitation, but in the very possibility of its being, of the immanent foundation of its life. The spider's web is once again one of those spaces of extension that are born of a space of life and exceed it, but so too are they spaces of living that specifically serve not only to allow life to stand forth from death, but also to actively engage and accelerate the process of degradation and disintegration that is also the process of nourishment and growth that we assign to the end of an individualised-life. The spider's web as a space of capture constitutes a space of life and death in which the death of one brings forth the life of the other through the enactment of a series of predator–prey, growth–decay, eaten–ate relations. The unfolding of life into death, and its acceleration through predation, reveals once again the tendential connectivity of the living and the dead, not only as a clearing of space for another, but also as death being integral to the possibility of life.

And this connectivity of the living and the dead through spaces of cohabitation, dwelling and co-flourishing, that is the commons of the living and the dead, is found in an array of animal dwelling-places. These dwelling-places do not only constitute a shelter and space within which life can exist, rather as dwelling-places they concern the very possibility of life and are given meaning through it, that is it is the active process of becoming that characterises these dwelling-places as dwellings at all. The termites' mound not only provides a material structure which termites exist within, as though it were merely an inactive shell or backdrop against which the living of the termite colony can occur, an empty and hollow space of finalist-death. These mounds do not simply house the colony, but crucially and importantly function in the transformation of energy.[138] As such, these built structures enact processes continuous with those of the physiology of the delimited animal organism and its metabolic processes, they function as what could be described as externalised organs, which is to say they form an element of the animal's organology. Thus it is not only the tool in relation to the human that stands before life, revealing its continual unfolding into death as an unfolding of the living beyond the limits of delimitation and into nothing-ness, but so too the web of the spider, the mounds of the ter-mites, the calcium of the polyps.

So in this way the spaces of death through and with which we dwell become continuous with those of life, revealing an *Extended Organism*[139] that undoes the opposition of the living and the dead whilst bringing the spaces of death and nonlife into an exten-sive organology. Such an extension to the organism's limits, one which unfolds its delimitation in a manner revealing its continu-ity with death, brings to light the manner in which that which is determined as inactive, dead and nonliving, functions within the very processes of life from which it is banished and, in forming elements of its possibility, dwells within life. So it is not that the living dwell within the dead, that spaces of death are manipulated by the living only from the perspective of life and only for the advantage of life, but just as much it is death that dwells within the living, and the ground of nonlife converges with that of life in a manner that confounds the delimitation of either.

So what then are the dwelling-places of the human? Are not our houses and huts, our tents and caves, our urban and rural environments alike, spaces of nonlife that give forth life? In par-ticular, the urban domain which so many people now inhabit reveals itself to us as a vastly complex ecosystem of life and death, one in which the extension of the organism occurs in the most varied, layered and complex ways — in the flowing of the sewers, the surging of electricity, the streams of traffic and tributaries of streets and roads, the transmissions and circulation of informa-tion and symbolisation, the capture, release and manipulation of vast libidinal currents. "Urban space gathers crowds, products in the markets, acts and symbols. It concentrates all of these, and accumulates them."[140] And in this gathering, this accumulation, we can identify the coming-together, the becoming-with, of life and death, the tendential connectivity of both.

However, the urban space in particular, in its position as a space of the absorption of excess and the eruption of endless accumulation, has so often become a space in which the tendential connectivity, this commoning between the living and the dead, has been concealed and marginalised under the figures of finalist-death, under the logics of opposition, rationalisation and fatalism. The continual purging of life, that is the absolute exclusion of the living, from the rationalism of nonlife appears as the impossible dream of modernism. The grand structures of the modernist dream stand within the urban as spaces of nonlife that attempt a violent silencing of the tendential interplay between life and death. As an architecture modelled on the opposition of the living and the dead, that is moulded in the image of finalist-death, the vast towers of modernism with their proud, tall straight lines and gleaming pristine surfaces deny the efficacy of nonlife other than as a rationally manipulated backdrop for life. The processes of decay and dirt are excluded from them, and every morning and evening people across the cities come to these spaces tasked specifically with cleaning away any remnants of life that might cling to these structures, with the attempted absolute annihilation of any nonhuman life form, microbial or otherwise, that might seek to dwell within these domains of finalist-death.

Of course this annihilation is never final or absolute, for no number of attempts could entirely remove the tendential connectivity of the living and the dead. The marginalisation of microbial life that manifests itself so clearly on the immaculate glass surfaces of the looming urban towers can never be total, and the continual reassertion of life within even those spaces so closely modelled on the notion of a finalist-death reveals the inescapability of the cohabitation of life and death. And what is more, the emergence of life upon these planes that sought to exclude them need not be the object of a collective neurosis of cleanliness in which life, to its own destruction, seeks to impinge upon itself.

Rather, these processes of decay and degradation, of life standing forth from its attempted exclusion, can become a matter of joy and affirmation as in the *Mouldiness Manifesto* of Hundertwasser.

> When rust sets in on a razor blade, when a wall starts to get mouldy, when moss grows in a corner of a room, rounding its geometric angles, we should be glad because, together with the microbes and fungi, life is moving into the house and through this process we can more consciously become witnesses of architectural changes from which we have much to learn.[141]

The urban domain, rather than being built to exclude life — that is, built in the image of a finalist-death of rationalism and opposition — is inescapably decaying, and it is this very decay that is an unfolding unto death that is also the springing forth of life. This springing forth of life is that of which the finalist tendencies of modernist architecture remains in denial, and which it seeks to continually exclude under the banner of rationalism. But this exclusion can never occur or find its absolute realisation, for the architectural domains from which exclusion is attempted already form elements of a vast ecology of extended organisms, that is they are already and inescapably continuous with life, as elements of an organology by which life faces death and death faces life; the living dwell and become-with the dead.

It is hoped that it is clear that in all these instances what is important is not that one builds in order then to dwell — that the spider constructs its web in order to dwell within it, that the termites build their mound in order to live inside, that the humans construct the urban domain only then to later inhabit it — it is not that building has dwelling as its goal.[142] Dwelling, that is becoming in life and death, existing as a durative-soul in continual becoming, connection and swelling, is anterior to building. To build we must dwell with the living and the dead, and we must share our becoming with them. To build we must, so to speak, inhabit the commons of life and death, as entities that appear delimited, but are in fact spread more and more thinly across a vast expansive domain of connection, collision and association. Dwelling does not come after building, for in building we dwell. We dwell with the so-called dead entities that we assign to the realm of technics and tools, and we cannot think of these apparently dead entities without thinking of their other side, that is their life and the life with which they are continuous. We cannot think the tool and yet ignore the hand just as we cannot think the hand and seek to ignore the tool. And tool and hand cannot oppose one another as exclusory opposites, just as the living and the dead cannot stand opposed to one another each as the principle of utter exclusion of the other.

Dreaming

Prometheus, the titan who would grant the mortals access to the trace and technics and in so doing bring about mortality and his own enchaining, also engaged the domains of anticipation and premonition through the space of dreaming. The dream, for Prometheus, could hold the power of foresight and prophecy. In telling his tale Prometheus declares,

> Then I distinguished various modes of prophecy,
> And was the first to tell from dreams what Fate ordained
> Should come about; interpreted the hidden sense
> Of voices, sounds, sights met by chance upon the road.[143]

This view of the dream as coming forth from divinity and revealing that which is as yet unknown recurs often. The dream here is taken to be an association to a beyond, a transcendence that represents the passage to a beyond and a temporality outside of singular duration and the myopia this perspectival limitation entails. There is an association to a transcendent-life, to a beyond of eternal and divine truth outside of the limits of the degraded temporal world. Such an understanding of the dream expresses the fact that the individual, in dreaming, is placed into connection with that which exceeds it and undoes its limits, that which brings forth an individualised tiny death as the disillusion of an interior. In the transcendence of the divine dream, the limits of experientially teleological temporality are undone and the divine eternity brings forth the future. In this way the limits of an individual are effaced under the banner of the sacred infinity that it can scarcely glimpse in the dream. But can we step forth into this beyond without a divine light to guide us; can we still handle the confronting of the beyond of finitude without an eternal sacred assurance?

It is not enough to dismiss this beyond with which the dream communicates as nonsensical, as the reminiscence of divine metaphysics and religious speculation. Rather, what is needed is a confrontation of this notion—that the dream communicates and articulates a beyond—without the hierarchical and all-too-human naïveté that would find a monotheistic pinnacle to the living, and likewise without an excessively individualised, bounded and enclosed all-too-human subject taking its place. But rather than being a beyond in the sense of a monist absolute truth, a nihilistic judger and knower of all that in turn effaces all, the beyond to which the dream communicates can be seen as that of an extensive connective communication. In such a way it would be the expression of an extensive connection of the durative-soul; its inscribed and inscribing singular multiplicity, and its entanglement with that with which it is implicated but always-already exceeds.

In this way the beyond to which the dream communicates would not be a beacon of truth, a source of premonition or epiphany with all the force of the One behind it. Instead, this beyond would unfold as the messy, entangled and knotted beyond of connective communication, a beyond that is infinite not as an absolute divine entity, but infinite in as much as it always exceeds any one finite individuality and in as much as it remains continually expansive through the becoming that communication is inseparable from. It is an infinite beyond in as much as communication, and proliferative connection, ensure becoming as the continual movement into a beyond on the part of a given individuality—the being of the between as the space of connective communication is becoming. In this way the dream articulates within the finite individual that which exceeds it, that which goes beyond it and that from which it cannot, try as it may, achieve severance.

The dream, as such, is less an individualised psychological structure that expresses the murky oedipal-ridden domains of the individualised unconscious than it is an articulation of the open whole within the limits of the individual. It is a point of communication between life and that which exceeds it, namely death. It is a point by which the living entity, as we saw earlier, "opens itself up to the opening of the world... inscribing itself within a temporal dimension that is irreducible and nonclosed."[144] The dream then becomes an articulation and further inscription of the passage of the durative-soul through a given individuality, and further, one that exceeds the consciousness we have of it. It exceeds the consciousness that we have of it not in the sense of a hidden unconscious of the individualised subject, but in the sense that both the body and thought surpass the knowledge we have of them[145]—we do not and cannot know what thought and bodies can do or how they are entangled. Quite literally there are more things in heaven and hell than dreamt of within or beyond philosophy. As such, this is not a reduction of the dream to individualised unconscious memory—quite the opposite, it is an undoing of unconsciousness and memory as deindividualised, extensive and connective, as implicated in that which exceeds any one individual and so brings about a tiny death of the living.

Take the patient in Freud's *Interpretation of Dreams* who describes hearing for the first time in a dream of the liquor *Kontuszówka*.[146] That which is forgotten, in the sense of something discarded by contemplation rather than in the sense of that which is lost by a knowing individualised consciousness, returns in the dream. But as with the forms of evolution this liquor remains present in absence for its absence, its forgetting, is itself an inscription as are the forgotten forms of now-evolved species. Likewise the recurrence of infantile memories in dreams discussed by Freud and Volkelt reveal the inscriptive and inscribing connection of the dream spaces that associate individualities with that which exceeds them, and in doing so bring life into communication with death. Forgotten forms that are central to thought are revealed in their absence and the boundaries of finitude become undone. The contemplation of the *Kontuszówka* by the dream reveals an inscription of durative-souls that exceeds the consciousness we have of it. We return to the Proustian exemplars of involuntary memory — the madeleine, the steeples of Martinville, the cobbled streets of Paris. A dream came to me; I dreamed, or I was dreamt?

It is not so much that the individual consciousness articulates the world through *its* dreaming, but more that the extensive world speaks through the dream. In the dream the finitude of bodies comes face to face with the uncanny infinity of the cosmos, but there is no divine truth or illumination to fall back on, only the complex entanglement of durations and their continual proliferation. It is not simply a case of a feeding of sense data through the body into the mind, as though the mastery of the mind over body that ensures Man as the pinnacle of an all-too-human life is the only possible means of durative experience, but of the continuity of thought beyond any one body,[147] the emergence of thought through communication, semiotic or otherwise. Do dogs dream? Kohn asks — and with a contemplative, forgetful and thinking *phusis* now unfolded before us, we can agree not only that they do, but also that they are dreamt; that is, they are entangled in extensive chains of communication and thought, through and from which the dream finds its articulation.

But what would such a deindividualised extensive dreaming reveal once removed and displaced from the calculative structures of dream analysis? We would be left with a domain that uncovers and confronts the finite body with a thrown entanglement that exceeds the consciousness one has of it, that far exceeds any one body's field of vision. This is an unconscious in the sense of exceeding the finitude of consciousness, of opening up not to *nihil* but *infinitum*, an unconscious of the bodies as much as of *noesis*. Here, the dream becomes understood less as a calculable, mechanised and functionalised standing-reserve awaiting the explication of the knowing analyst, but as a connection of individualised-life to that which it is not, of the finitude of bodies to the infinite connective beyond, that is to death. The *Kontuszówka* was not simply forgotten by the I-sayer's isolated subjectivity, but rather it was a knot in their thrown entanglement that exceeded their consciousness of this entanglement, an entanglement that is always beyond the reach of the myopia of thought and bodies.

There can be read the articulation of such a beyond in the cosmology of the Australian Dreaming—but it is no longer a case of locating the social meaning behind the Dreamtime, as though the illusory veil of myth and cosmology held beneath it the truth to be discerned by the knowing eye just as the psychoanalyst uncovers the truth of the individualised dream in the murky depths of the subject's unconscious. Rather, being that "time out of time" and "everywhen" from which all entities—people, animals, trees, lakes and mountains—come, the Dreaming forms a cosmological and ontological domain in which the connective entanglement of bodies beyond the limits of perspectival myopia is embraced and harnessed. The Dreaming is not conceived as a fictional domain, but as a different order of reality, one that nevertheless permeates the world and is productive and active within it.

It would be wrong to see the link between dreams and Dreaming as being based in the unreal or illusory nature of both. The Dreaming does not express and articulate an illusory reality, the question of reality does not even come into its ontology in such terms. Rather, as with the dream when laid bare, deindividualised and released of the structure of calculative analysis, the Dreaming reveals profound truths regarding the entanglement of bodies in the world, and does so particularly forcefully due to its revealing in the manner of a calling forth beyond the limits of a mechanised and calculated standing-reserve. The Dreaming gives us a "poetic key to reality"[148] — not a calculated functionalised reality, but a creative poetic framing, a poetic revealing of truth, a *poesis*.

In the Dreaming we find an ontology that sees "man, society and nature, and past present and future... at one within the same unitary system."[149] These domains violently separated in the episteme of finalist-death, and those dimensions isolated by telic-temporality, are inseparable through the Dreaming. That which emerges comes to be through the Dreaming whether it be an all-too-human social order, the artist's new song, or the rise of mountains. The Dreaming associates finite bodies to the infinite, the temporal to the eternal, to the courses of the starts, the primordial origins of fires, the fall of sorcery, the rising of the hills and the flowing of rivers. As with the dream, the Dreaming connects the telic-temporality and finitude to that which is always-already.

In their thrownness bodies are always-already entangled with that which exceeds them, with that persistent and frightful nothingness that is not *nihil* but the beyond of delimited being. The child was always-already existent in the Dreaming, alongside the flourishing of the crops, the vast expanses of the skies and the endless depths of the ground, the potentiality of their becoming was whispered of in the movement and passages that came before, and is echoed in those that follow. This is not a case of determined fatalism, but of infinite entanglement, connection and its endless reverberation. Many of the rules, patterns and forms were "already ruling in the Dreaming."[150] The all-too-human worlds of morality always-already existed in the Dreaming. As with the gods of the many pantheons, adultery, betrayal, murder and greed continue as powerful forces in the time out of time of the Dreaming. Moral codes and customs are always-already at play as much as they are always-already transgressed — the very transgression that brings forth the ruptures and tearings that in turn call forth moral orders.

Thus we may link the Dreaming and dreams through the space time of the always-already, a time outside of time that is nonetheless always-already implicated in the passage of bodies, in the formation and proliferation of their durative souls, of the very multiplicity that affirms their becoming, the always-already that is the space of non-finite, non-telic entanglement. The Dreaming speaks of connective entanglement, of the knotting of lines[151] and bodies, of their powerful communication, of the shared voices of gods and mortals. The standing forth of bodies, becomings and forms from the Dreaming, thus emerge from this perspective as a poetic revealing, a creative worlding.[152] It is a revealing that asks not of reality as a prefigured standing-reserve, but of a poetic autosatisfaction, a flourishing, a contingent emergence of potentiality.

But this is not a standing forth in the sense of a coming-into-reality from the beyond of a separate metaphysical plane that hovers above the world and passes judgment and claims jurisdiction over the here-below. The beyond of the Dreaming is not the beyond of a transcendental plane of the divine, of salvation or heaven or hell, nor is it of the transcendence of platonic forms[153] — it is once more a beyond in as much as a finite body is always implicated in that which exceeds it, in the numerous deaths through which it passes and which dissolve its temporary and contingent delimitation, in as much as individualised-life overspills continually into death. There is no beyond of salvation for the ontology of the Australian Dreaming, no redemption or punishment of above or below, no prophet or saviour, no sickness unto death, only a beyond in the sense of a nonfinite time out of time, the always-already of dreaming, a beyond of the finitude of bodies in the thrown entanglement of dreams. The beyond of life is not a *nihil*-death, but once again we say it is an *infinitum*, a non-finite space of an entanglement that has always-already begun. This beyond of the dreaming is not made beyond by rupture or hierarchy, it is not the beyond of divine Neo-Platonism, it is a beyond that is entirely continuous with that which it is beyond. Here entanglement "and continuity, not man, is the measure of all."[154] No one gets to be Man.[155] There is no moral rift "between what life *is* and what men think life *ought to be*"[156]; as with Dreaming, both finitude and the beyond have always already transgressed not only moral codes, but also one another.

And Say the Dead Responded?

Now, can we still claim to stand before the dead as the active end of two poles of mutual exclusion? Can the living still stand in life at the exclusion of death? The violence by which the pinnacle of the living excludes all other forms of life as lesser, and the dead as less than *nihil*, denies the legitimate activity and efficacy of anything that is not permitted to enter its interiority, and yet one merely needs to turn this interiority upon itself in thought to find that it can no longer maintain this separation. In powerful communication, a communication that undoes the bound of language and moves beyond the mastery of Man over his tools, life confronts its inescapable continuity and connectivity with the world finding that, to the shock and dismay of its own hyperbolic naiveté, it is not as distinct from those entities that it sought to demean as it had hoped. The active interiority of thought can no longer be maintained as outside and distinct from the chains of becoming and the commons of the living and the dead with which it is continuous. Both contemplation and forgetting unfold into nothing, into a beyond that is of infinite connection. No longer can the dead be denied the possibility of response.

And yet this denial of response beyond the closure of individualised-death is something that we have become so greatly accustomed to that its reality appears as obvious. What is the death of the other, or for that matter even the death of the self, if not the closure of their possibility, that is the limits of their efficacy and activity? When we mourn for the loss of the other, when we experience that violent affect caused by another's passing and the fits of despair and unbearable horror that it carries with it, we have often become custom to thinking of this process as a matter of "coming to terms with" the passage of the living to the domains of nonlife, that is with the absolute and final end-of-life. As Freud writes, the process of mourning is:

> carried out piecemeal at great expenditure of time and investment of energy, and the lost object persists in the psyche. Each individual memory and expectation in which the libido was connected to the object is adjusted and hyper-invested, leading to its detachment from the libido.[157]

Here, the death of the other is the loss of a beloved object, and the mourner stands in relation to the deceased as an active interior subject gazing upon a now entirely inactive and inefficacious dead-thing. To mourn is to embark on a process of gradual separation in which the living stand apart from the dead and continue life without them. The persistence of the dead in the realms of the living that the violent call of mourning enacts is, according to the psycho-analyst, only temporary—the extension of duration and the continuation of the durative-soul in its collision with other bodies, the powerful communication between them and the affection of the other is only temporary, awaiting that moment when the work of mourning may be complete and the object is detached from the libido.

And yet we have seen that the beyond of life is a beyond with which life dwells. To separate out the living from the dead would be an act of violence against both, for the space of technics, of dwelling, of dreaming have all shown the forceful call of the other and of the nothingness of *infinitum* within the domains of life to the extent that to speak distinctly of the domain of life begins to lose its meaning. That powerful communication that speaks through us and that permeates the perceived limits of a being, whether it is through the call of involuntary memory, the sexual union or the dream, reveals to us our eternal entanglement in the infinite commons of the living and the dead—whether exteriorised to the technical object or the dwelling-place, the spaces of nonlife which the living engage with, shape, create and transform do not remain entirely external to life but return and respond within it.

There always remain the possibilities of return. There is always an opening up of individuality onto that which is other than it. There is always an extension of duration. Such extension and opening is found not only in the space of technics and dwelling, but so too does it call us in the violence of mourning. The death of the individual is but the deintensification and deterritorialisation of a specific series of durations, the diminishing of a specific material locus of connective intensity. "An actual death is simply a more violent instance, from a certain point of view, among the many deaths and resurrections that a person suffers."[158] This locus and this duration are always connective, and so the tendency towards death always appears alongside a tendency towards the living, one that maintains connection with the living, that brings about affect in the living, and is extensive throughout the domain of the living. Death is not the outside of life. It is not an externality that may deform and degrade life. Death is not the bastard sibling of a legitimate life. It is rather a mode of connection, affection and transformation. The loved may die, but their death is not final.

> To go on speaking of this all alone, after the death of the other, to sketch out the least conjecture or risk the least interpretation, feels to me like an endless insult or wound—and yet also a duty, a duty toward him. Yet I will not be able to carry it out, at least not right here. Always the promise of return.[159]

Derrida mourns Barthes. He does so with the promise of return, one might even say the insistence of return. The death of the other stays other, the alterity by which the other was known in life persists in death, the difference by which this individuality was known remains difference, and yet it shares a becoming-with, an extensive and connective co-flourishing that is the intermingling and collision of durative souls. In the passage towards death, the loss of vitality is never absolute, for effect and affect remain beyond the finitude of bodies. The death of individualities brings endless wounds, but they are wounds that will not heal—or at best will scar, and in their scarring or their refusal to heal the transformative insistence of life finds one of its cruellest forms, precisely in its interplay with death.

And so in mourning, and the confrontation and interplay of life and death that it articulates, there can be no hyper-investment that will be absolute, that will result in detachment, for there is always the promise of return. The singularity of durations has already merged, they have been caught in connection, the anticipation and protention of which shatters any linearity that would allow one to end, for detachment to be complete. The connection of durations, which are unavoidably both multiple and singular, is unavoidable just as is the play between life and death. It cannot be that mourning overcomes the loss of the object, for the object is never lost and was never only an object, it was never only external. The mingling of duration, the intersection of flows, the inescapable web of connectivity, insists upon the impossibility of absolute loss. Insisting that they were with us and will always be with us; that we lived with them and will always be of them; that life was shared and shaped together and will never be lost. Death cannot be reasoned in terms of total detachment for such detachment will not come. "[W]hoever thus works *at* the work of mourning learns the impossible — and that mourning is interminable. Inconsolable. Irreconcilable."[160] The living do not leave the dead behind them for their connection has always-already been forged.

> To live, by definition, is not something one learns. Not from oneself, it is not learned from life, taught by life. Only from the other and by death. In any case from the other at the edge of life. At the internal border or the external border, it is a heterodidactics between life and death.[161]

Life learns from death, and death from life — it is a matter of interplay, of tendency. And so the dead cannot be denied the possibility of responding, of speaking through us, affecting us, moving us and reverberating throughout the worlds of the living. Even when the exclusion is sought, their return is insistent — the microbe returns to even the most sterilised of modernist tower blocks and the advancements of technics are folded into the so-called noetic interiority of life. Indeed, if we were to characterise our current situation in terms of the preceding discussion we might begin to consider that what is at stake in the great political, ecological and anthropological questions of our time is precisely the echo of the insistent call of the dead.

The spaces of capital and of technicisation, articulated as functional instrumentalisation and mechanisation — that is, as the constitution of a standing-reserve that has caused the disenchantment of reality and denial of life and death's tendential connectivity through a mode of revealing that leaves nature as an area of Man's conceiving and a research object[162] — deny this call of the dead. And yet the realities of our current condition are increasingly making such a denial unfeasible. For what is at stake in the Anthropocene is in many senses the undeniable reality of the call of the dead. That it would be the liberation of carbon[163] that is particularly characteristic of this time is unsurprising, for instrumentalisation of the dead in the burning of their fossilised remnants, in the incineration of vast quantities of oil, gas and coal, is once more the response of the dead and not only the extension of their duration — that is the continuation of the collision and collusion of durative-souls — but also a mode of powerful communication at a scale of general economy before which the human mind reels in horror, apparently incapable of comprehending.

The mass incineration of the remains of the once-living that has fuelled industrialisation and technical evolution at an unprecedented rate has manifested itself as a mode of revealing with little respect for either the dead or the living. Through such incineration,

> the energy concealed in nature is unlocked, what is unlocked is transformed, what is transformed is stored up, what is stored up is, in turn, distributed, and what is distributed is switched about ever anew. Unlocking, transforming, storing, distributing, and switching about are ways of revealing.[164]

And these modes of revealing present the living to the dead and the dead to the living through an endless gathering together and bringing forth in an inseparable unity. But through the mechanisation and instrumentalisation of the dead, that is their reduction to mere-thing, to a malleable standing-reserve that is subject to the mastery of the living, their power is ignored and the persistence of their call dismissed. Thus the continual denial of the effects of the Anthropocene and the mass devastation of global ecosystems emerges as an effect of the inability to heed the voices of the dead, to acknowledge their agency, and their significance for the living in locating the possibilities of co-flourishing. And it is this instrumentalisation that enframes *phusis* as a standing-reserve, that is as a delimited domain of research known as nature, that manifests once again in the denial of the agency of technics, in the exclusion of the tool and the technical from the domain of action that is reserved for the living.

But we must take care to try and not be misunderstood here, for we do not mean to suggest that this denial of life and death's tendential connectivity is inherent to all technics, but rather to what appears to us now as a certain mode of *Gestell*,[165] that is an enframing of becoming in the image of finalist-death, a framing of life without gradation and transition and without connectivity to death, and an enframing of death as the total exclusion of life. It is this enframing that reveals becoming as disenchanted, as shying away from powerful communication and the articulation of the sublime as the impossibility of maintaining discontinuity. For as with the arts, the unfolding and revealing of technology is the unfolding of the Sublime, that experiential moment where taxonomised faculties overspill and collapse, where the interiority of the human subject is undone amidst a transcendent connectivity that violently and forcefully compels one beyond oneself in a surge of powerful communication. Thus life moves beyond itself and is placed into communication with death as an absolute dissolution of interiority and separation. Technology is Sublime in the sense that it provides a point of connectivity, a source of powerful communication that challenges the contingent limits of beings and forces them to enter the endless becoming of the between. And thus code is poetry for it undoes the isolated interiority of the existential subject, unfolding and exteriorising it to call forth truthful connectivity and emergent form — the code brings forth beings and taps into undercurrents of powerful communication that exceed the stratified formality of its language.

It is precisely the functionalisation, stratification, mutual exclusion and opposition that the image of finalist-death enacts that leads us to a disenchanted reality in which the interplay and conflict of *phusis* has been enframed as and reduced to a standing-reserve that produces the violent system of judgment in which the dead and living are excluded from communication with one another. For it is this denial that produces the political ecologies of life and death that are run through with thanatophobic tendencies, in turn producing thanatophobic organologies modelled in the images of finalist-death. This denial of the dead by the living brings forth the insistent call of the dead all the more violently and forcefully, and the more this call is ignored the stronger it responds. It is the revenge of Gaia who, confronted with the rampant arrogance and hyperbolic naïveté of Man, calls forth warning after warning leading up to the point whereby the confrontation of the tendential connectivity of life and death will violently enforce itself. This is the meaning and significance of the Anthropocene — the revenge of Gaia manifesting itself as the inescapable and flagrant call of the dead.

CHAPTER 4

Political Ecologies of Life and Death

Political Economy and the World of Things

What is the *world of things* that political economy presents us with? What do we see when we are confronted with the products of labour, in whatever form they may take? Surely not the result of human's work upon "nature," if by nature we understand a realm that is outside and around us, the backdrop, set and stage upon which the drama of a narcissistic anthropology unfolds. There is a twofold nature to the so-called labour process of the worlds of political economy: those of the "social realm" — of living, breathing, interacting entities — and those of the valorisations of capital — that siphon off, extract and remove from the living, breathing "social world" the nonliving forms of capitalistic value and use. It is this latter domain, which seeks to spread itself across everything, including the living social realm, and enforces its interpretation of all, that constitutes the *world of things*.

This is a *world of things* that is actually divorced from things in the world and things of the world, it is a *world of things* in which the creation of value becomes the despotic interpreter of all-things. This *world of things* is impoverished, and sings through the tonalities of finalist-death — it denies the life of which it was born, that is it enforces its interpretation of thinghood — valorisation, commodification, estrangement. This *world of things* becomes the tyrannous interpreter of life and death, and in its delimitation of a narrow *world of things* reduced to principles of functionality, utility and value, reifies absolute death. These are the two parallel worlds of political economy, enforced by schisms and double-binds, the two worlds of life and death, of living-labour and dead-labour. From the perspective of this *world of things*, all becomes a mode of existence for the dead forms of capital — the body of the worker, the thoughts of the general intellect, the flows of resources, the growth of plants, the sediments of the deceased now fossilised—and there is nothing that cannot undergo perspectival transformation by such a *world of things*, modelled on the figures of finalist-death, to become nothing more than an extensional mode of existence of capital.

Political economy expresses and produces a thanatophobic-organology and anthropology which enforces a schism between the realms of the living and the dead, leaving life cowering in the face of an image of death that is monstrous and dominating. The realms of dead *things*, objects that are merely the products of labour or the natural resources on which labour works, emerge as entirely other than the realm of the living, and in the somnolence of their death and nonlife are thought to function and operate at the service of their living masters. There is no continuity or contiguity, and it is this lack of continuity and contiguity that leads to the dominance of dead forms over living, the dominance of dead-labour, capital and balance-sheet-based values. Dead forms, presented as entirely devoid of vitality, are the primary concerns of economics and political economy. Life becomes little more than an externality. Economic thought concerns itself with products, capital, labour-units, all of which are reduced to rationalised, mechanised and functionalist units of management and measurement. In this way economism establishes itself as the *science of finalist-death*.

The *world of things*, the world of absolutely dead forms, mirrors the world of vitality from which it draws its power, but it does so in a manner whereby its own reflection is not visible. It is vampire-like in its extraction of vital force, and in its concealment of its own reflection within the very mirror it uses to interpret the world entirely whilst also denying its existence or the possibility of alternative viewpoints. In establishing itself as the *science of finalist-death*, economism allows this mirror to be bypassed and ignored, presenting the extracted reflection as the absolute and only reality, through the mechanism of a *principle of functional reality*. And in this bypassing and concealment of the play of mirrors, the *science of finalist-death* draws forth the aphasic foundation of science to the benefit of its own power and domination. In this way it enacts a kind of arrogant scientificity that conceals and forgets the conditions of its formation to the extent that "if it admitted it had no foundation, no reality would subsist – from which it derives a power that induces it to calculate: it is a decision that invents reality."[166] Rising itself up above the world of dead forms over which it claims powers of control and management, the system of judgment that economism spreads across what it presents as the Real becomes the despot and ruler of the living and the dead. But in doing so the tendential connectivity of the living and the dead is denied, with the effect that both are degraded and denied communication with the other. Instead, the figures of finalism are granted a power above all else, to the extent that the dead are denied life and the living are denied death for they are caught in the mechanistic system of finalist-death become scientific.

It is in this way that we may reconsider Marx's statement that "[t]he *devaluation* of the world of men is in direct proportion to the *increasing value* of the world of things."[167] It is less that "men" are degraded in relation to the *world of things*, but more that the living, and by tendentially connective implication so too the dead, are devalued and degraded in inverse proportion to the swelling of the sphere of finalist-death that political economy enacts. And so we are left surrounded by the appearance of a *world of things* that has been hollowed out of any vitality by the schisms of political economy. It is a *world of things* that ensures that the dead appear to the living as estranged, and in so doing are able to dominate them. This *world of things* is one that is presented to life as being its opposite, and in so doing it is permitted the ability to syphon off life and vitality to see it added to an ever-growing graveyard of finalist-death and fatalism. Labour and work are objectified to the point where objects devoid of vitality produce more objects, the dead are impoverished to the level of calculating mechanism, and in so doing the living are placed in their service. The souls of objects and the souls of people are reduced to figures on a balance sheet, to productive elements in a world characterised by mechanism and utility, to an enframing as a standing-reserve and the reduction of *phusis* to nature.

Once more, Marx writes "[t]he worker puts his life into the object; but now his life no longer belongs to him but to the object;"[168] and so too the vitality of the object, its singularity, soul and becoming, are reduced to no more than an absolutely dead form, a form run through with finalist-death. This is one of the many bases of estrangement — that of the hollowing out of both life and death, and the vital interplay between them, the schism and bifurcation of their tendential relationship, allowing each to confront the other as an alien entity, an entity apparently as far from the other as could possibly be. The object of labour appears external to the labour that saw it brought into being, and the realm of the dead is denied any relationship to the realm of the living other than that of tireless, brutal extraction and domination.

Marx was well aware of the tendential relationship that rests beneath the schism of political economy, the schism that would place a separated realm of the living in the service of a realm of mechanistic, finalist-death. Marx knew that "labor cannot *live* without objects on which to operate,"[169] not only in the sense of that extensive domain beyond the given individual that provides the means of reproduction and sustenance, but in the deeper sense of the integral connection of bodies, the multiple mesh of durations and extensions, without which no body could be formed. Marx knew that "plants, animals, stones, air, light, etc.... constitute a part of human life and human activity."[170] It is this connection that political economy conceals in its separation of the living and the dead in the favour of an impoverished realm of absolutely nonliving entities, entities reduced to a finalist-death, and that is hidden in the denial and concealment of the play of mirrors. In its tireless production of value as utterly dead form, as form separated from life and enacting dominance over life, capitalist political economy reduces vitality to production, survival, utility and mechanism. Both the living and dead are devalued in favour of a system of schisms and separations that ensures that both are reduced to little more than cogs and wheels in a calculating, generalised and disenchanted reality. This is the condition of soullessness, the sigh of the oppressed, the heart of the heartless that Marx identifies as expressing itself partly through religion.[171] It is this extraction that serves a machinery and system that seeks to marginalise vitality in favour of survival, that reduces the power of action of the increasingly soulless worker, and likewise homogenises the realm of the nonliving — of the environmental and technical extensions — on the basis of their utility to capital. Capital is a form that, in its absolute separation of the living from the dead, reduces both to its mortified, undead foot soldiers.

The schisms capital enforces, that separate life from itself and death from itself, ensure that the more that labour engages with the realm of the nonliving, the more its power of action is reduced, the more this schism is enforced and strengthened. Both worker and object become servants to an ever-growing sphere of finalist-death. The souls of objects and workers are both masked, minimised and devitalised. We stand before a means of production and system of technics that holds power over us and yet our denial of this power grants it all the more power, and likewise we stand before a mechanised nature in the midst of Gaia's revenge and confront it as impotent and incapable to intervene. The strength of the sphere of capital accumulation, of the thanatic amassment of degraded nonliving forms, rests upon an inverse decreasing of vitality—both living and dead are robbed of their efficacy and power of action as ethics, the art of living, and so too dying, are forgotten. The worlds of nonliving and living entities are forced to confront one another as oppressors: both are reduced to little more than units of value production that serve no other purpose than the accumulation of fatalised forms, for no reason other than their continued dominance. Workers can only feed themselves through tireless labour, objects are only of importance in relation to this labour, animals are reduced to objects of value, and the extensive environmental domain that Spinoza sought as God or nature becomes scarred as any vital tendency is diverted into the flows of capital. All are put to the service of "alien, divine or diabolical activity." [172] We see estrangements of both *self* and *thing* as all are put to the services of the dominant abstractions of capital, utility and normalised, homogenised value.

The World of Work

What does it mean to work in this context of a bifurcated political economy? Of what do we speak when we consider the act of working to be an "intrinsically human" act? What does it mean to work even when capital is not the only determiner of action, the sole despot and ruler? In *Eroticism* Bataille claims that the taboos of death, the terror of the excess, transgression, violence and disillusion of individuality that death enacts emerges alongside the world of work. The world of work brings the functionalisation to the world that allows for the banishment of the dead and death to the non-effective and inactive space of the nonliving, to the functionalised and rationalised domain of nature. What is confronted in the corpse is the violence that is not only the death of one individuality, but of the endless unfolding of life into death, the many deaths through which all life must pass as the very condition of its possibility. Thus in the world of work, "[w]e must run away from death and hide from the forces that have been unleashed."[173] In work, this space of death is functionalised and denied efficacy, it is expelled from the world of life and assigned to a space over which Man can claim mastery, but nonetheless what is endlessly confronted is the persistent and terrifying call of the dead, its continual and continuous reverberation within the world of the living. Thus the arrogance of Man, in remarkable bad faith, seeks to claim efficacy even over death, that is it seeks to aim at its denial.

The world of work permits the bypassing of the persistence and continual articulation of death in life. In the functionalisation of reality, the beyond that is death, the beyond that denies the grip of reason is brought into the space of order and calculation, and its violent excess, its insistence on the disillusion of individuality and life become ignored, marginalised and excluded from the world of the living. Thus death appears as an unknowable terror, the call of the night, the horror of our inevitable demise—"death is like disorder in that it differs from the ordered arrangements of work"[174]—for when we confront death, when we confront the corpse, we are confronted with an excess which refuses subordination to the world of work, the world of functionalised and ordered action.

In this bypassing, and the exclusion of death that it enacts, we lose sight of the true entanglement of the worlds of life and death—their unity. We come to understand the world of work as that which Man can dominate, but what we fail to approach is the domination work holds over us. The denial of the efficacy of death and its endless violent imposition upon us, that is its continual undoing of the domains of the living, of the self, of the subject of the individual organism, grants it the power to dominate us all the more, to bring the inevitable transgression of life by death into the forbidden and ignored spaces of an exclusory morality. In identifying with the world of work, in making it the *telos* of life and reducing becoming to the chain of cause and effect, life becomes blind to the violence of death, violence in the sense of an excess and undoing of delimitation, that nevertheless persistently permeates the living and cannot be removed. The violence of the unknowable movement away from the world of work, the world of order, rationality and functionalisation, is concealed but not removed for no life can persist beyond the passage of the tiny deaths that in fact sustain it and grant it the possibility of flourishing.

So what then is the world of work? It reveals itself as the space that allows for the exclusion of death in the reduction of the excess that lies beyond delimited entities and the grip of reason to the *world of things*. It is an endless struggle against a death that is reduced to an entropic nihilism. In its banishment of death, the world of work constitutes the substratum of substance as the inactive domain capable of manipulation by the efficacy of life—it is in this sense a space of an all-too-human judgement that denies its inevitable entanglement with death, that permits for the springing forth of salvation and the eternity of life. In so doing, it displaces that subjective sovereignty that can stand before the tragic entanglement of life and death and grasp it, placing life in the service of death and death in the service of life in a vitalism that so too unfolds as thanatism; a sovereignty that confronts the limits of the flesh and laughs, a sovereignty that stands forth amidst the unfolding of the living and the dead and finds a unity of opposition that was extinguished in the overcoming of Heraclitus by Parmenides.

In the world of work, a world that constitutes death as *nihil* is found; it is a world that in so doing denies vitalism, and denies the flourishing of the living and the dead through its expulsion of the insistence of death. So too does the world of work constitute one of those earthly utopias that the scheme of telluric-death constituted as its beyond, as its eternity, as its telic scheme that would subordinate the durative passage of individualities to the salvation of the transcendent beyond. To gaze upon one's flesh and see death as much as one sees life is to confront the inevitability of this object of nonknowledge, to no longer stand before it in terror or sickness; it is to stare upon one's mortality as an inevitability that no longer incites horror, but quite to the contrary permits the flourishing of one's passage, one's durative soul, one's many lives, many births and many deaths in an active determination.

The compulsion to work is a compulsion to deny death, and in so doing to deny life, to deny the unfolding of birth and death that unfolds as the tragic enactment of living, of a body's ability to act, of ethics. "The community brought into being by work considers itself essentially apart from the violence implied by the death of one of its members."[175] This world of work then, is not only the narrowly defined world of the Economy, of Labour, Exchange and Value, it is rather the space of calculation and prohibition, the space of exclusion to the violence that undoes individuality and so too life, excluding the spaces of sex, the spaces of defecation, the spaces of death. It is a domain of calculation that brings together a rationalised and functionalised community to stand against the threat of violence that can undo order, that constitutes reality and forgets its role in that constitution, and denies any enchanted reconstruction of reality through this aphasia.

Dead Labour, Proletarianisation and the Finalist Means of Production

In his ethnography *From the Enemy's Point of View*, Eduardo Viveiros de Castro states that the Araweté word *mani*, to die, refers broadly to losses of memory and consciousness, *kaaki hã*. The examples he uses within the specific context of the Araweté include "drunkenness from beer, tobacco narcosis, shamanic accidents (when the gods knock out the shaman), [and] traumas such as illness and grave wounds."[176] What is struck at in this understanding of death and what it means to die, at least in the context of the current ideas, reveals profoundly the tendential connectivity of life and death, and further the manner in which this tendential connectivity is not supressed in *epistemes* that to some extent operate outside the grip of finalism. For the Araweté, reference to dying and death is not reserved for the finalist occasion of an individualised degradation and rupture; there are many deaths, and many gradations and shades between the living and the dead. The Araweté thus acknowledge the numerous tiny deaths through which all of us pass, with which we all dwell, and which are indissociable to living.

The loss of memory and forgetting, temporary or otherwise, and transformations of consciousness are understood here as tiny deaths, as moments in which the living are compelled beyond themselves and thus into the nothingness that exists at the limit of one's being, that is the nothingness that is simultaneously death, *infinitum*, multiplicity and becoming. There are numerous phases of transition and gradation, it is not a matter of rupture, or opposition, of severance or total discontinuity. To draw out the difference between this conception of death, and that enacted through the *science of finalist-death* with its bifurcations, double binds and oppositions, we can turn to another process of memory loss, that is the process of proletarianisation.

Proletarianisation is not only a process of material dispossession and the creation of a huge social class reliant on wage-labour, but it is also, and quite crucially, a loss of memory and knowledge. This process is highlighted throughout Marx, and more recently re-examined by Stiegler.[177] The loss of livelihoods and the conditions of material sustenance that so-called *primitive accumulation*[178] enacted brought with it a loss of *savoir-faire*. In the widely studied case of the enclosure of the English commons, the dispossession of the commoners from their means of reproduction destroyed entire bodies of knowledge and produced a class dependent on wage labour.[179] As the commoners were separated from their land, and the spheres of production and reproduction became bifurcated, entire systems of vernacular knowledge straddling what would become the gendered separation of production from the reproductive were lost.

Subsequently, the industrial revolution and the development of machinery unfolded as a vast acceleration of grammatization, understood as "the history of the exteriorization of memory in all its forms."[180] The loss of knowledge with which the process of proletarianisation began, that is the dispossession of both the material basis of sustenance and the knowledge that came with this, was magnified and accelerated as the gestures of the workers became folded into the machinery of capital. The domain of living labour was folded into the space of dead labour, but in a way that denied and short-circuited their connectivity and continuity, that is the affective and tendential relationship that one supposedly separated domain has with the other.

Thus a means of production grew which encased within it the lost memory and knowledge of its proletarian operators. And so extensive and universal did this means of production become that the encasement of memory and knowledge within its means of production extended also across the body of the worker, making even the apparently living, breathing organism go on "[l]iving as a sacrifice of life."[181] And so, through this ever-swelling sphere of dead labour — a sphere of dead labour devoid of continuity, and modelled in the image of finalist-death — "[t]he multitude has surrendered to the somnolence of production, living the mechanical existence — half-ludicrous, half-revolting — of *things*."[182] The body of the worker, their knowledge, memory and vitality, became reduced to the half-life and half-death of a *world of things* devoid of continuity with the worlds of the living.

Thus the formation of a finalist means of production enacted a reduction of the worker, their numerous tiny lives, tiny births and tiny deaths, to the *world of things*. As the *savoir-faire* of the worker became transformed by the system of political economy and its *episteme* of finalist-death to stratified and generalised labour power it became encased in the equivalency and inter-facability of capital's code. "From a bearer of tools and a practitioner of instruments, the worker had himself become a tool and an instrument in the service of a tool-bearing machine."[183] The technical system, now reduced to a finalist means of production modelled on staticity, discontinuity and generalised exchangeability, becomes a mortified reservoir that captures the flow of tiny deaths, the flows that unfold in the development of technics as the processes of transindividuation between milieus of tool and hand, are siphoned off and denied the possibility of continued interplay and vitality. Thus the life of the worker, in as much as they are both a worker and labour-power, is reduced to a life at the service and under the domination of the image of finalist-death.

And so, with approaching the domain of technics reduced to the means of production that is in the mode of nature and the standing-reserve, the *science of finalist-death* denies the continuity and vitality of technical sphere, that is its inescapable entanglement and tendential gradation in connection with the living. And so proletarianisation—a loss of memory and knowledge in its becoming-folded within the technical means of production—unfolds as a continual confrontation with death; but modelled as it is in the scheme of a finalist-death, economism denies this continual unfolding of life onto that which is other than life, and so increases the domination of both all the more furiously.

Here, in the realm of machinery and in the realm of automation—that is, in the foldings of knowledge and memory encased within the means of production, but denied their status as components of the chain of living thought that also encompasses the nonliving—"is the domain of the dead object, the commodity, which objectifies human activity reducing it to a cognitive automatism."[184] Under the image of finalist-death, both the living and the dead are denied as the dead are relegated to the domain of object and thing, and the living, in the same movement are denied their vitality and connectivity with the dead; the denial of connectivity being the denial of life and death, for it is the denial of their unity.

And so it is in this context that we now understand Bifo's proposal that alongside a Vitalpolitik, "we should speak of 'thanato-politics' (from the Greek *thanatos*,' meaning death): the submission of intelligent life to the dead object, the domination of the dead over the living."[185] The politics of life must be studied and understood alongside, and in inescapable connectivity with, a politics of death. But by a politics of death, here we understand a politics that becomes sensitive to the commons of the living and the dead, that is to the processes of negotiation, interaction and shared understanding of the living by the dead and the dead by the living. A politics of death would be one that not only orients us towards a means of understanding and engaging with individualised-death, that is the degrading of the organism that is so often locked away in sterile medicalised spaces, or banished under the signs of abhorrence and illness, or only to death as one's ownmost potentiality. Rather, such a politics of death would become sensitive to the means in which the dead are engaged with and understood by the living, in the relationship to tools and technics, in the ecological positioning of the dead, in the enframing of *phusis*, in the ever-unfolding processes of decay and forgetting, in the tiny deaths of self, the dwelling of life in death, and the denial of death and life. A politics of death would be a politics that listened for the response of the dead. In short, it would be a politics that seeks to engage with rather than banish the dead, and become aware of the many nuances and variations of the relationships between the living and the dead.

Let us return to the Araweté. In addition to bringing forth the tendential connectivity of life and death — the numerous tiny deaths and births with which life and death swell and through which they pass — the Araweté consider that people do not truly die, that is, as we said earlier, "[a]n actual death is simply a more violent instance, from a certain point of view, among the many deaths and resurrections that a person suffers."[186] This certain perspective, from which death is merely a more violent continuation of the continual unfolding of lives and deaths, is that of the dead themselves — the perspective of the dead is granted efficacy and the ability of some kind of phenomenological perception, something that was excluded from the domain of the dead by the Aristotelean hierarchy of souls. And so such a conception of death and the dead appears to allow for the response of the dead, that is for the reverberation of their call to be heard and felt within the worlds of the living; it is a politics of death that is not one of opposition and mutual exclusion, but of gradation, tendency and conversation; it is a politics of death that listens for the call of the dead.

Exchange, Debt and Death

So now, what do we mean when we speak of exchange within the context of these systems of political economy and their bifurcations of the living and the dead? It is a notion that has become infused with the logics of the *science of finalist-death*; it has become a notion of ever-increasing staticity, a notion of continually rebalancing finalities, a notion devoid of the emergence, flux and fluidity of soulful movements. The so-called markets of today, where every transaction occurs in an absolute equilibrium, where the books are immediately balanced, where investment is repaid with interest, where borrowing is met with debt, are entirely removed from exchange. In them, exchange is dying a finalist-death, a death that seeks to expunge life, a death that, knowing nothing of life, cannot be death. What then do we mean by exchange?

It is once more a matter of moving beyond. Ex- to become ex-ternal, to ex-ile, to ex-it, is a way to ex-ist — that is to be out-side, to out-reach, to make and do (-ist) with the out-side and of the out-side and so to adhere to out-side with the out-side — to ex-ist. Exchange then is always a going-beyond, a pushing of boundaries, a traversing of limits, an unfolding of interiorities and a foray towards the infinite nothingness. It is a movement beyond limits, an ex-scape of that limit and so too an ex-termina-tion of that limit. Such traversals show the transience of bounda-ries, the partiality of their separation, the continual fleeing of the horizon, and the impossibility of clearly thinking an inside-out-side. It is the ex-termination of the limit, bringing about an emer-gence of difference, the unspringing of the new, a change, a trans-formation. It is a matter of ex-change.

Ex-change, then, is a moving-beyond and transformation borne of engagement with this beyond, it is an emergence of dif-ference through the passage of a singular duration, a duration that is always concretising, increasingly singularising and mul-tiplying, connecting and individuating. It is a transformation resultant of the transcendence of a limit, the continual insist-ence of contingent transience. To ex-change is to modulate, it is unbalanced precisely by the fact that it does not become equal, it does not balance; it always goes beyond and always seeks exten-sion and connection. Ex-change then is inherently imbalanced, it is disequilibrium, and cannot simply be recorded formulaically upon balance sheets.

This is revealed as we approach giving; that is, a mode of ex-change that has not been submitted to the tyranny of a final-ist-death, or at the very least resists reduction to its staticity and generalised interfacing. Nothing is balanced in the giving of gifts and the sacrifice this entails. To repay a gift entirely equally is to destroy the gift, it is to expunge the given and giving, to annihilate by oppositional violence any sacrifice encased in the thing given. To recognise the gift as gift, to balance the given with a counter-gift, is to annul the gift and reduce it to nothing, to the completion of an equation, to the full turning of the circle. It is to remove it from the domain of ex-change and place it within the domain of exchange demarked by economism as the universal equivalency of like for like, the balancing of mechanised standing-reserves. The gift is a gift precisely because it is unbalanced, because it is not immediately repaid, because it does not pertain to an equational balancing. A gift is a gift because it does not belong to the domain of quantitative equality—it is of *différance*, always a deferral and a difference.

But the gift is not a difference in the sense of a simple taxonomy of equalities, not in the sense of a universal general equivalent or in the sense of the mere interfacing of units through one code, it is not a difference marked by a unitary measure at its centre that orders all difference around that centre. And likewise it is not a deferral in the sense of a mere intention to pay later, in the promise to meet the given with gift at a future-present. The difference of a gift is a difference of radical ambiguity, that is of an indeterminacy that undoes the very notion of the gift as an object given and rather unfolds it as "a remainder that is not nothing since it goes beyond everything,"[187] a remainder that compels beyond the stratification and finalism of economistic systems, opening unto a proliferation of potentiality and connection, a beyond that is confronted as an ever-fleeting horizon.

The gift remains a gift by operating beyond, that is in the space of the remainder that is out of time, that places time out of joint, and in operating beyond it splits open the balanced figure of the circle. In this way it permits an insistent refusal to become "engaged in a symbolic, sacrificial, or economic structure that would annul the gift in the ritual cycle of debt."[188] So there is no longer a logic of the gift other than one of interruption, disequilibrium and a remainder that operates beyond the exchange cycle of subjects and objects, a logic that could hardly be called logical. This rupture and imbalance shatters the finitude of economism, and its taxonomies of finalist-death, revealing a mode of exchange that no longer functions according to an inevitable return and circularity, but a boundless and unpredictable swelling, a reaching toward the beyond, a foray into the infinite, and so too a foray into nothing. Thus the gift engages a mode of ex-change, a going-beyond and a transformation, that draws upon and dances with the living and dead alike in its foray towards the *infinitum* of the anticipated horizon, that is it confronts and stands before the tendential connectivity of life and death as it stands before and confronts the infinite. In this way the gift enters misosophical domains where the stratification of economism's received wisdom is shattered by an untimely time out of time.

The gift is a gift because it is not met with a figure of exchange that is the figure of total return—it is not a matter of balancing or equivalency, but of imbalance. In this way the gift is of a mode of debt quite alien to what we have come to understand as debt—it's indebtedness is not that of a balanced equation, but of a continual disequilibrium, of a vital interplay that swells and collides, of a series of flows and intensities that cannot be encapsulated or enframed as a standing-reserve. It is an ex-change and indebtedness that integrally cannot be framed as standing-reserve due to the interfacement with the horizon of the beyond toward which it swells. In this way the gift is a "radical forgetting"[189] of its own phenomenality as gift, it is a forgetting that upsets the circular figure of exchange and tears apart the equilibrium of the balance sheet. Thus the forgetting of the gift is also the thought of the gift; the forgetting of differences characteristic of thought pointed to by Borges[190] is here rearticulated with an indeterminacy so radical that its own forgetting is forgotten.

To give a gift is to play with the radical indeterminacy and ambiguity of the remainder, of that which is beyond and cannot be given in time; it is to move into the beyond and to relish it, never looking back for the point where the circle would return to its originary moment. In this way the gift institutes a mode of debt that is a mode of imbalance — not simply an imbalance between two delimited entities, subjects or I-sayers, but an imbalance that is foundational to the interplay of the living and the dead, that is the continual back and forth through which life is constituted in death and death in life. Thus the materiality of the things given can become seen as contractions of intersubjective spacetimes[191] in as much as what they draw upon, what they engage with, what they attempt to call forth is the being of the between that was identified as becoming and that continually propels itself towards an ever-fleeting horizon. In this way the materiality of given things are not the gift, for in the instances that they are recognised as gifts, that is in their presentation as a gift, they would annul the element of the gift. What the gift achieves is a kind of refusal, a refusal of delimitation and a refusal of equivalency; it compels us towards a becoming that refuses to be encapsulated and finds its radicalism within spaces of ambiguity, imbalance, conflict, rupture, uncertainty and impossibility, spaces that are also the *terra incognita* of misosophy.

And so, love, life, time and death give through us, they are not given by us, for we cannot own them any more than we can identify and delimit them — thus they are gifts in the purest sense in that they are never given as gifts, they are never present as gifts and are never recognised as gifts. Their presentation is not in the present and thus their presence is not present, but nevertheless the reverberations of their givenness are felt throughout the living and the dead. In this way to give is to give that which one does not own, and such a giving institutes an imbalance that is not one of equivalence just as it is not one of simple deferral, of a promise to pay later, not now, in a future-present; rather it is an imbalance of the most primordial kind, an irresolvable conflict within *phusis*. To even think of repaying in kind love, life or death is to entirely miss the significance of these horizons, and their unity.

The gift, thus, is not met by a return — rather, ex-change is always marked by difference, by a fluctuation, by a movement beyond the thing given and between the giver and the receiver. The giver and receiver are always in fluctuation, always in ex-change — the giver receives in connection and extension and the receiver receives likewise. It is always a gift of *hôte a hôte*.[192] The guest and host, the host and guest, give to one another, but never equally. To return to the gift an equality is to disembowel the gift, is to remove its given, is to recognise it as gift and so dissolve it. It is not simply a strengthening of social ties, an advancement of alliance; it is a transformation, a moving-beyond, a reaching toward the horizon.

So, we see how the conception of exchange that is now common sense, the conception of exchange proposed and maintained by the *science of finalist-death*, is far removed from the gift, from ex-change, and from the primordial debt of the imbalance and conflict of *phusis*. For if equivalency and return are key to economism, "[i]f the figure of the circle is essential to economics, the gift must remain *aneconomic*;"[193] that is it must interrupt the figure of the circle understood as the return to equivalency and instead capture and propel the remainder, the excess, the movement beyond, the pursuing of the horizon. So the exchange of which political economy speaks, the interfacement of exchange-value and the reduction of all to this central measure of value, enacts a balancing act that minimises and ignores the radical ambiguity, indebtedness and imbalance of ex-change as articulated in the going-beyond of the gift. And so the modern mode of debt that now ensnares so much of the world, that is the balancing of the sheets characteristic of capitalist exchange, enacts a levelling-out which robs ex-change of its imbalance, movement and thus the very vitality and radical ambiguity that brought forth its power from the horizon of the beyond. And so in this way capital denies life and life denies capital through the reduction of ex-change and debt to little more that the staticity of a finalist-death, to the equilibrium of the balance sheet.

The Persistent Call of the Dead

The horizon with which we began, that of the domain of the dead and the eternal fleeing of life towards death, has now been unfolded before us as a domain of inseparability from life. Death has not been revealed in the mode of an entity, that of a given defined and delimited thing that could be demarked as death, but has revealed itself as a flow of tendency, a flow which is variously found to be connective or, at the other extremity, found to be denied and banished. The figure of finalist-death has stood forth as a barrier to the tendential connectivity of vitality, that is to the endless upsurging of life and death and the continual unfolding of the one unto the other. Thus vitality itself has unfolded as the connection of these two supposedly separate domains. Vitality is no longer the exclusion of death. It is no longer the negation of the dead and the privileged domain of life, but is the inescapable unity of the living and the dead, the implication of each in the possibility of the other.

What has been at stake in the attempted blurring of the line between the living and the dead, and in the interrogation of the barrier that enacts a separation between absolute-life and finalist-death, has been the continuity of living and dying, the gradation and transition between tiny deaths and tiny births. Thus what has been sought, and what has unfolded in a space of confusion and nonknowledge, has been a space of an unconscious that is the myopia of knowledge and philosophy in its inability to bring into logical and coherent rationality the entanglement and collusion of bodies and the movement towards the infinite that is found in the anticipation of death. And so, in the uncanny space of surrealistic nonknowledge and misosophy, what is revealed is something that denies articulation by rationalised discourse, namely "[t]he profound unity of these apparent opposites, birth and death."[194] In this profound unity we have confronted the interior of life's inability to maintain the barrier between its inside and its outside, we have confronted the violence that in denying the efficacy of the dead so too denies the efficacy of the living through a shattering and compartmentalising of vitality.

We have approached a perspective where the limit of life and the limit of death no longer stand opposed to one another, but are drawn into interplay with one another and unfold as tendencies acting upon one another. If we now reconsider the notion that "[l]ife is above all else a tendency to act on inert matter,"[195] we can also see that the inverse is true, namely that death is a tendency to act upon the living. Death acts upon the living in the anticipation of one's ownmost potentiality, in the fleeing of individualised-life towards its own degradation, but this degradation acts in turn upon the living in the provision of the decay from which life springs forth. Death acts upon the living in the space of the technical object which, as an exteriorisation of life unto a space of nonlife, folds itself back upon the living and enters into affective relation with it. Death acts upon the living in the dissolution of interiority, in the space of absolute contradiction that rests at the infinite depths of the self, in the problematic of individuality, in the contraction of contemplation and forgetting, in the persistent reminders of connectivity that were encountered in taboo, sex and excrement, in the experiential content of the Sublime as the overspilling of discontinuous faculties, in the call of the dead as the revenge of Gaia.

So now, when we understand life as being continuous with a machinic phylum, the phylum that Deleuze and Guattari uncovered in their examination of metallurgy, we must also understand the inverse — the continuity of death as the reverse tendency of matter's vitalism. What is uncovered in the notion of the machinic phylum is the vitality of what becomes defined as the inert or dead. As they write,

In short what metal and metallurgy bring to light is a life proper to matter, a vital state of matter as such, a material vitalism that doubtless exists everywhere but is ordinarily hidden or covered, rendered unrecognizable, dissociated by the hylo-morphic model. Metallurgy is the consciousness or thought of the matter-flow, and metal the correlate of this consciousness.[196]

The machinic phylum uncovers life's connectivity with that which is deemed to be nonliving in a manner comparable to the contraction and contemplation of matter and conditions in the wheat.[197] In this instance, the example of metallurgy is particularly informative due to the position of metals as some of the most powerful catalysts other than organic enzymes, and as catalysts they bring about vital transformations at a chemical level of analysis, "[t]hat is, a catalyst intervenes in reality, triggers effects, causes encounters that would not have taken place without it."[198] What metals reveal in this process is precisely their efficacy, that is the efficacy of what would so often be confined and banished to the domain of death and nonlife, an efficacy that is hidden, covered and rendered unrecognisable by the barrier erected by finalist-death. And as questions emerge regarding the metabolization of iron by bacteria,[199] the question of delimiting the boundaries allowing for the conditions of a form of life is rearticulated and complexified.

If life is continuous with the space of nonlife, if they are part of a continuous machinic phylum, that is if metals enter into the chains of vitality, then the spaces of nonlife, in the inverse, become continuous with those of the living in a manner by which the tendency to act on inert matter is reversed and rearticulated through the tendency towards death as a tendency toward the dissolution of the living. And so vitalism is reasserted, but no longer in the sense of the absolute affirmation of life and at the expense of the total negation of death, but rather as the endless interplay, the continual back and forth, of the tendential relationship between the living and the dead.

So what do we make of this tendential unification? What do we make of the unfolding of life unto death and death unto life that is vitality itself, and how do we articulate this unity? This unity articulates itself variously and heterogeneously. It was found in the questions of bio-individuality, but also in the domains of phenomenological experience and the existential self. What the parallels in attempting to define the limits of the organism and the continual unfolding of the self unto other reveal is precisely this unity, that is the inseparability and tendential connectivity of life and death.

We may turn to the words of a writer who we mentioned once at the start of this text, and who whilst he has not been continually referenced throughout, has been resting behind the words as they have unfolded and has been present upon a certain intertextual surface. In articulating this unity, Novalis writes that "[d]eath is the Romanticizing principle of our life. Death is minus, life is plus. Life is strengthened through death."[200] Death is a tendency to act upon life, and life a tendency to act upon death, and their unity is assured through their interplay with one another, their continual unfolding unto one another. Life is romanticised through its conversations and engagements with death, and death is equally romanticised through its interplay with life.

This notion, of the unity of life and death as articulated through a romantic principle, was encountered, albeit on a differing plane, in the experience of the sexual union as that moment where the boundaries of discreet individualities can no longer be maintained naturalistically or phenomenologically. Likewise, in the experience of the sublime as the total overspilling of taxonomised faculties and in the experience of self as associated to the infinite, we encountered the unity of life and death in the propulsion towards a nothingness that was not *nihil*, but an *infinitum* which would forever exceed the ability of supposedly delimited consciousness to grasp it. What these moments revealed was the place of love, that is of the sensation of beholdenness to others, and the agony and violence this calls forth, as the unifying and romanticising principle of life and death. Once more Novalis writes,

> [t]he heart is the key to the world and to life. One lives in this helpless condition in order to love — and to be beholden to others. Through imperfection one becomes open to the influence of others — and this influence of others is the purpose.[201]

Through love the impossibility of maintaining boundaries is asserted and the opening up to the world and to the influence of others is affirmed alongside the tragedy that this entails. Thus love is not merely some kind of well-wishing feeling of comfort and a total lack of animosity, but rather, in its opening up of individuality and its becoming vulnerable, sensitive and interdependent, it is an experience of agonising violence, it is an experience that compels interiority to dissolve itself, and to pull forth from the inside that which must be brought forth to the outside. In this sense, that of the sense of love being a compulsion to go beyond and enter the agonising space of uncertain infinity, "the urge towards love, pushed to its limit, is an urge towards death."[202] And it is this compulsion to the beyond articulated in love that carries with it "the same thirst for losing consciousness and the same after-taste of death that is found in the mutual desire for each other's body."[203] The urge beyond one's self, the urge beyond individualised-life, the urge even beyond life in general, is a foray towards death, it is a confronting of death as the disillusion of boundaries and the resolution to stand forth in the tragic conflict of *phusis* as myopic.

This call towards death that is also the call of the dead will never diminish, and the persistence of its call can only become more violent the further it is marginalised and ignored, that is the more we practice "the exclusion of the dead and of death."[204] This exclusion of the dead and death amounts to a form of neglect for the commons of life and death; it is a denial of their interdependency and a failure to appreciate the need to cultivate conditions of co-flourishing. It is a failure to approach thanatopolitical questions and their implications. The response of this call is felt in the dominance of dead labour over the living, of the finalist means of production's reduction of all to a static image of finalist-death and the rearticulation of vitality by this means of production as "the indifferent consumption of life and death, the mutual neutralization of life and death in sur-vival, or death *deferred*."[205] Thus the call of the dead here articulates itself through the codes and bifurcations of political economy, through this institution of a mechanised world of things and the reduction of even the bodies of workers to a standing-reserve.

And this articulation of finalist-death runs through the worlds of the living and the dead, denying their co-flourishing and tendential interplay. The development of the technical sphere, now short-circuited and handed over to the *science of finalist-death*, is left at the mercy of a dominating image of death, one that denies the efficacy of the tool and its interplay with the milieus of life. Technology stands before us as something foreign, something encased, something over which we believe we should have mastery, and yet have the recurring uncanny sensation that it is master of us. It is not that technology dominates us or enslaves us, nor that technology alienates or estranges, but rather that technology handed over to the image of finalist-death, that is denied entry to the domain of vitality, serves to further the domination of a mode of death that is final and absolute, a mode of death which paralyses us and leaves us unable to even articulate questions regarding our connectivity to its milieu. This is what is understood now by the notion of technology as an enframing and a reduction of *phusis* to a standing-reserve—namely that it is this enframing, an enframing that emerges from modes of finalist-death and the staticity and opposition this implies, that leads to technology appearing so dominating to us rather than it being inherent to the technical sphere itself.

But we should be clear that for us this enframing is not restricted to the world of political economy nor the technical milieu, but is far more deeply rooted than that, and leads us to a situation where the violent and persistent call and response of the dead surfaces as the standing-forth of a new geological era: that of the Anthropocene. That *phusis* became enframed as nature, and nature as a mechanised and instrumentalised domain of Man—a domain that could be explained and systematised, a domain that became entirely disenchanted and subject to the *principle of functional reality*, a domain in which the fossilised remains of the dead become no more than a storehouse for the explosive productive capacity of capital—has led to a situation where our political ecologies are unable to comprehend the response of the dead that we are now facing, in the form of ecological catastrophe. The significance of the Anthropocene is that of the persistent call of the dead, a call that refuses to be silenced, and that promises the further it is run from the greater it shall pull life back.

The reversal of this enframing, that is an opening up of the tendential connectivity of the living and the dead appears now as of crucial importance to the flourishing of vitality, that is the co-flourishing of the living and the dead. To attempt to approach the ecological, political and economic earthquakes of our time without learning to hear the call of the dead seems futile, for it is the very ignorance of this call, its attempted silencing, that grants the figures of finalist-death such power. The power of finalist-death is a power capable of paralysing vitality, it is a power that seizes attempts to think of alternatives in its binary system of opposition and exclusion, that leaves us caught in the grasp of an apparent fatalism and inevitability. This is what, in the context of the current writing, articulates itself as *capitalist realism*,[206] the fatalism and inescapability of the image of finalist-death. And this relentless realism, the realism that demands staticity and opposition, that demands the nihilism encased in finalism, reduces resistance to a game and pantomime, "a fist fight between portraits."[207] We are left in a situation where the general intellect appears paralysed under the weight of the image of death that has come to dominate it, where *savoir-vivre* is handed over to the system of immaterial labour,[208] and where life stands before itself as something alien to itself, something devoid of vitality.

But we should not allow the weight of the question to press so heavily upon us, for in spite of the apparent universalising tendency of capital and of the *science of finalist-death*, neither can ever be absolute. The unity of life and death that is vitality can never be entirely excluded if only due to the inescapability of the fact that "[d]eath is not an event within existence because it is the very possibility of existence."[209] Whilst the figures of finalist-death may attempt to attain universality, death cannot be ignored—it is rather a matter of how long it will take the arrogance of Man to subside, and how long it will take for us to learn to hear what is the continual and persistent call of the dead. There is always the possibility, in fact we might even say the eventual inevitability, of a rupture—we saw this in ex-change and the gift, but also in the space of dreaming, the work of mourning and the sexual union. These ruptures will not disappear; they open up the very basis of delimitation and opposition into connections that compel the supposedly discrete individuality beyond itself. And such ruptures exist elsewhere and release themselves in the lines of flight, escaping from the excessively hardened refrains of finalist-death.

For likewise, we cannot deny, and indeed we have continually seen, that there exist modes of enframing, systems of metaphysics and phenomenological experiences that powerfully undo the apparent opposition and exclusion of life and death — the domains of gifts and sacrifice, the experience of the sublime, the imbalance of ex-change, the collusion of bodies and durative souls. And what is revealed in such domains is precisely the tendential connectivity of life and death; their unity as vitality. So we are left with as many questions as we began with, and in fact it would be hoped more. How do we stand forth and orient ourselves towards death beyond the grip of finalism? What modes of experience are necessary for us to undo the hyperbolic naïveté and arrogance of Man? How can we attune our hearing to listen to the persistent call and response of the dead? If life and death unfold as the flux and flow of vitalism itself, what is the significance of these two movements? If no longer the limit, does *death* reveal itself as the horizon of *life*? And inversely, does *life* reveal itself as the horizon of *death*?

BIBLIOGRAPHY

Aeschylus (1968) *Prometheus Bound, The Suppliants, Seven Against Thebes, The Persians*, London: Penguin

Aristotle (n.d.) *De Anima* (On the Soul), online at http://www.perseus.tufts.edu/

— (n.d.) *Nicomachean Ethics*, online at http://www.perseus.tufts.edu/

— (n.d.) *Physics*, online at http://www.perseus.tufts.edu/

Badiou, Alain (2012) *Being and Event*, London: Continuum

Bataille, Georges (2001) *The Unfinished System of Nonknowledge*, London: University of Minnesota Press

— (2007a) *The Accursed Share: Volume I*, New York: Zone Books

— (2007b) *The Accursed Share: Volume II & III*, New York: Zone Books

— (2008) *On Nietzsche*, London: Continuum

— (2012) *Eroticism*, London: Penguin

— (2012) *Literature and Evil*, London: Penguin, e-book

Baudrillard, Jean (2011) *Symbolic Exchange and Death*, London: Sage

Berardi, Franco Bifo (2009) *The Soul at Work: From Alienation to Autonomy*, Los Angeles: Semiotext(e)

Bergson, Henri (1998) *Creative Evolution*, New York: Dover

Borges, Jorge Luis (1998) *Fictions*, London: Penguin

Brasier, Clive (1992) "A Champion Thallus" in *Nature*, vol. 356, p. 382-3

Campagna, Federico (2013) *The Last Night: Anti-work, Atheism, Adventure*, London: Zone Books

Camus, Albert (1975) *The Myth of Sisyphus*, London: Penguin

DeLanda, Manuel (1997) *The Machinic Phylum*, online at http://v2.nl/archive/articles/the-machinic-phylum

Deleuze, Gilles (1984) *Kant's Critical Philosophy*, London: The Athlone Press

— (1988) *Spinoza: Practical Philosophy*, San Francisco: City Lights Press

— (2004) *Difference and Repetition*, London: Continuum

— (2006) *Nietzsche and Philosophy*, London: Continuum

Deleuze, Gilles & Guattari, Felix (2004) *A Thousand Plateaus*, London: Continuum

— (2011) *Anti-Oedipus*, London: Continuum

Derrida, Jacques (1994) *Given Time: I. Counterfeit Money*, London: University of Chicago Press

— (1994) *Spectres of Marx*, London: Routledge

— (1998) *Of Grammatology*, London: The Johns Hopkins Press

— (2001) *The Work of Mourning*, California University Press

Descartes, Rene (2003) *Meditations and Other Philosophical Writings*, London: Penguin

Epicurus (n.d.) *Letter to Menoeceus*, online at http://www.epicurus.net/en/menoeceus.html

Federici, Silvia (2009) *Caliban and the Witch: Women, the Body and Primitive Accumulation*, New York: Autonomedia

Fisher, Mark (2009) *Capitalist Realism: Is There No Alternative?*, London: Zero Books

Freud, Sigmund (1997) *The Interpretation of Dreams*, London: Penguin

— (2005) *On Murder, Mourning and Melancholia*, London: Penguin

Fromm, Eric (2004) *Marx's Concept of Man*, London: Continuum

Garcia, Tristan (2014) *Form and Object: A Treatise on Things*, Edinburgh: Edinburgh University Press

Guattari, Felix (2008) *The Three Ecologies*, London: Continuum

Guattari, Felix & Rolnik, Suely (2008) *Molecular Revolution in Brazil*, Los Angeles: Semiotext(e)

Haraway, Donna (1991) *Simians, Cyborgs, and Women: The Reinvention of Nature*, London: Free Association Books

— (2008) *When Species Meet*, London: University of Minnesota Press

Heidegger, Martin (1977) *The Question Concerning Technology and Other Essays*, London: Harper & Row

— (2000) *Introduction to Metaphysics*, London: Yale University Press

— (2010) *Being and Time*, Albany: State University of New York Press

— (n.d.) *Building Dwelling Thinking*, online at http://mysite.pratt. edu/~arch543p/readings/Heidegger.html

Heraclitus (n.d.) *The Fragments*, online at http://www. heraclitusfragments.com/

Hundertwasser, Friedensreich (1964) *Mouldiness Manifesto*, online at http://www.hundertwasser.com/english/texts/ philo_verschimmelungsmanifest.php

Huxley, Thomas Henry (1852) *Upon Animal Individuality*, online at http://alepho.clarku.edu/huxley/SM1/indiv.html

Ingold, Tim (2007) *Lines: A Brief History*, London: Routledge

— (2015) *The Life of Lines*, London: Routledge

Jobert, A. C. G. (1846) *The Philosophy of Geology*, London: Simpkin, Marshall and Co., Stationers' Hall Court

Kant, Immanuel (2012) *Anthropology from a Pragmatic Point of View*, Cambridge: Cambridge University Press

Kierkegaard, Søren (1989) *The Sickness Unto Death*, London: Penguin

Kitarō Nishida (1987) *Last Writings: Nothingness and the Religious Worldview*, University of Hawaii Press

Klossowski, Pierre (2009) *Nietzsche and the Vicious Circle*, London: Continuum

Kohn, Eduardo (2013) *How Forests Think: Towards an Anthropology Beyond the Human*, Stanford: University of California Press

Lacan, Jacques (2008) *Ecrits: a selection,* London: Routledge

Latour, Bruno (2007) *Reassembling the Social: An Introduction to Actor-Network-Theory*, Oxford: Oxford University Press

Lazzarato, Maurizio (1996) "Immaterial Labour" in *Radical*

Thought in Italy: A Potential Politics, Micheal Hart & Paolo Virno (eds), p. 133-147

Lefebvre, Henri (1991) *The Production of Space*, Oxford: Blackwell

Leroi-Gourhan, André (1993) *Gesture and Speech*, London: The MIT Press

Lienhardt, Godfrey (1978) *Divinity and Experience: The Religion of the Dinka*, Oxford: Clarendon Press

Lucretius (n.d) *On the Nature of Things*, online at http://www.perseus.tufts.edu/

Marx, Karl (1843) *Contribution to the Critique of Hegel's Philosophy of Right*, online at https://www.marxists.org/archive/marx/works/1843/critique-hpr/intro.htm

— (1844) *Economic and Philosophical Manuscripts: Estranged Labour*, online at https://www.marxists.org/archive/marx/works/1844/manuscripts/labour.htm

— (1986) *Capital: Volume One*, London: Pelican

— (1993) *Grundrisse*, London: Penguin

Munn, Nancy (1992) *The Fame of Gawa: a Symbolic Study of Value Transformation in a Massim (Papua New Guinea) Society*, London: Duke University Press

Myers, Fred R (1991) *Pintupi Country, Pintupi Self*, Oxford: University of California Press

Nietzsche, Friedrich (1968) *The Will to Power*, New York: Vintage Books

— (2003) *Beyond Good and Evil*, London: Penguin

— (2003) *The Birth of Tragedy*, London: Penguin

— (2006) *The Gay Science*, New York: Dover Publications Inc.

Novalis (1988) *Hymns to the Night*, New York: McPherson & Company

— (1997) *Philosophical Writings*, Albany: State University of New York Press

Plato (n.d.) *Apology*, online at http://www.perseus.tufts.edu/

— (n.d.) *Phaedrus*, online at http://www.perseus.tufts.edu/

Plotinus (1991) *The Enneads*, London: Penguin

Proust, Marcel (2000) *In Search of Lost Time Volume V: The Captive and the Fugitive*, London: Vintage

— (2000) *In Search of Lost Time Volume IV: Sodom and Gomorrah*, London: Vintage

— (2000) *In Search of Lost Time Volume VI: Time Regained and a Guide to Proust*, London: Vintage

Saint Augustine (1984) *City of God*, London: Penguin

Sartre, Jean-Paul (1947) *Situations I: Essais Critiques*

Schopenhauer, Arthur (1969) *The World as Will and Representation, vol. 1*, New York: Dover Publications

Serres, Michel (2007) *The Parasite*, London: University of Minnesota Press

Smith, Myron L, Bruhn, Johann N. & Anderson, James B. (1992) "The fungus Armillaria bulbosa is among the largest and oldest living organisms" in *Nature* vol. 356, p. 428-31

Spinoza, Baruch (1910) *Short Treatise on God, Man and His Wellbeing*, online at https://archive.org/details/spinozasshorttre00spinuoft

— (1992) *Ethics, Treatise on the Emendation of the Intellect and Selected Letters*, Indianapolis: Hackett Publishing Company

Stanner, WEH (1979) *White Man Got No Dreaming: Essays 1938-1973*, London: Australian National University Press

Stiegler, Bernard (1998) *Technics and Time: The Fault of Epimetheus*, Stanford: Stanford University Press

— (2013) *What Makes Life Worth Living*, London: Polity

— (2013), *For a New Critique of Political Economy*, London: Polity

Tarde, Gabriel (2012) *Monadology and Sociology*, Melbourne: re. press

Thacker, Eugene (2010) *After Life*, Chicago: University of Chicago Press

The Good News Bible (1976) London: The British and Foreign Bibles Society

Turner, J. Scott (2000) *The Extended Organism: The Physiology of Animal-Built Structures*, London: Harvard University Press

Viveiros de Castro, Eduardo (1992) *From the Enemy's Point of View: Humanity and Divinity in an Amazonian Society*, London: University of Chicago Press

Wark, McKenzie (2014) *The Birth of Thanaticism*, online at http://www.publicseminar.org/2014/04/birth-of-thanaticism/

Wark, McKenzie (2015) *Molecular Red: Theory for the Anthropocene*, London: Verso

Waterfield, Robin (2009) *The First Philosophers: The Presocratics and the Sophists*, Oxford: Oxford University Press

Watkins, Julie (1990) "Kierkegaard's View of Death" in *History of European Ideas*, 12 (1), pp. 65-78

Weiqiang, Li, Beard, Brian L. & Johnson, Clark M. (2015) *Biologically Recycled Continental Iron is a Major Component in Banded Iron Formations*, online at http://geoscience.wisc.edu/ICP-TIMS/wp-content/uploads/2015/08/Li_et_al_2015_PNAS.pdf

Whitehead, Alfred North (2004) *The Concept of Nature*, New York: Prometheus Books

NOTES

1   Novalis (1988) *Hymns to the Night*, p. 21
2   Bataille, Georges (2001) *The Unfinished System of Nonknowledge*, p. 197
3   *Op. Cit.*, p. 119
4   Guattari, Felix (2008) "Culture: A Reactionary Concept?" in *Molecular Revolution in Brazil*, p. 25
5   Nietzsche, Friedrich (1968) *Will to Power*, p. 291 §540
6   Yorck von Wartenburg quoted in Heidegger, Martin (2010) *Being and Time*, p. 383
7   Aristotle (n.d.) *Nicomachean Ethics*, 1115a.26
8   *Op. Cit.* 1115a.27-30
9   Aristotle (n.d.) *Physics*, VI:9
10   Plato (n.d.) *Phaedrus*
11   Stiegler, Bernard (1998) *Technics and Time*
12   Plato, *Op. Cit.*, 276a
13   *Op. Cit.*
14   Plato (n.d.) *Apology*, 40c
15   Garcia, Tristan (2014) *Form and Object*
16   Heidegger, Martin (2010) *Being and Time*
17   Novalis (1988) *Hymns to the Night*
18   These two apparently opposing notions are discussed widely in a range of guises but are particularly clearly expressed throughout the works of Kierkegaard (see, for example, *The Sickness Unto Death*; or for an overview of Kierkegaard's discussions concerning death see *Kierkegaard's View of Death* by Julia Watkins—published in *History of European Ideas* vol. 12). It goes without saying that these two conceptions of death do not encompass all, and very few if any can fully be brought under the banner of one, but they do perhaps represent two dominant approaches within what might be

referred to as "Western" thinking on death.

19 Heidegger, Martin (2010) *Being and Time*

20 see Aristotle (n.d.) *De Anima* (On the Soul); and Waterfield (2009) *The First Philosophers*, p. 164-192

21 Heidegger, Martin (2000) *Introduction to Metaphysics*

22 Aristotle (n.d) *On the Soul*, Book 1, Part 2

23 Lucretius, *On the Nature of Things*, 3.370-3

24 *Op. Cit.*

25 Aristotle, *On the Soul*, Book 2, Part 2

26 *Op. Cit.*

27 Nietzsche, Friedrich (1968) *The Will to Power*, p. 268-9, §485

28 Aristotle, *Op. Cit.*, Book 1, Part 5

29 *Op. Cit.*, Book 2, Part 1

30 *Op. Cit.*, Book 1, Part 3

31 Nietzsche, Friedrich (2003) *Beyond Good and Evil*, p. 32

32 Plotinus (1991) *The Enneads*, Part 1, Chapter 2

33 *Op. Cit.*

34 Saint Augustine (1984) *City of God*, Book 8, Part 2, p. 510

35 Kierkegaard, Søren (1989) *The Sickness Unto Death*

36 Saint Augustine, *Op. Cit.*, p. 210

37 Revelations, 2, 11

38 Saint Augustine, *Op. Cit.*, p. 510

39 Epicurus (n.d.) *Letter to Menoeceus*

40 It is important to acknowledge here the sinister work that continues to be enacted under the banner of Man, as well as the potential dangers in using the term now even critically. The use of the term Man here is not intended as any form of endorsement of the violence enacted by this notion, but rather the opposite is aimed for. What I hope is revealed by the use of this term is the way in which the notion of Man has established a masculine hierarchical pinnacle, under which all those assigned as "other" have been subordinated. In *When Species Meet* Donna Haraway shows how "others" have

been opposed to "Man", and how "[t]he rhetoric that connects categories of the oppressed in these programs is not subtle (prisoners, animals, the disabled, women in jail, black men, strays, etc.)" (p.65). The historical mechanisms that continue to enact this violence are complex, and their examination deserves its own attention, but in the context of the current work what is acknowledged is the way in which the category Man assigns those that are excluded from its definition to hierarchical positions that effectively deem them to be lesser forms of life. It is this hierarchisation that I hope to capture in the use of the term "the arrogance of Man."

41   Jobert, A. C. G. (1846) *The Philosophy of Geology*, p. 30-1

42   Nietzsche, Friedrich (1968) *The Will to Power*, p. 14

43   Haraway, Donna (2008) *When Species Meet*, p. 79

44   *Op. Cit.*, p. 79

45   Aristotle (n.d.) *De Anima* (On the Soul) Book 1, Part 4

46   *Op. Cit.* Book 1, Part 5

47   Nietzsche, Friedrich (1968) *The Will to Power*, p. 271, §490

48   Smith, Jason in Berardi, Franco Bifo (2009) *The Soul at Work*

49   Spinoza, Baruch (1992) *Ethics, Treatise on the Emendation of the Intellect and Selected Letters*, pt. 5 pr. 23, p. 213

50   Proust, Marcel (2000) *In Search of Lost Time Volume V: The Captive and the Fugitive*, p. 458

51   Bataille, Georges (2008) *On Nietzsche*, p. 177

52   Deleuze, Gilles (2006) *Nietzsche and Philosophy*, p. 36

53   Nietzsche, Friedrich (2006) *The Gay Science*, p. 119, §276

54   Spinoza (1910) *Short Treatise on God, Man and His Wellbeing*

55   *Op. Cit.*

56   *Op. Cit.*

57   Schopenhauer, Arthur (1969) *The World as Will and Representation*, vol. 1, p.253; see also *Fourth Vyasa Sutra*

58   Descartes, René (2003) *Meditations and Other Philosophical Writings*, p. 62

59   Kant, Immanuel (2012) *Anthropology from a Pragmatic Point of View*

60   *Op. Cit.*, p. 15

61   *Op. Cit.*, p. 59

62   Heidegger, Martin (2010) *Being and Time*

63   Nietzsche, Friedrich (2003) *Beyond Good and Evil*, p. 146 §146

64   Bataille, Georges (2008) *On Nietzsche*, p. 177

65   Sartre, Jean-Paul (1947) *Situations I: Essais Critiques*, p. 143

66   Bataille, *Op. Cit.*

67   Bataille, Georges (2007b) *The Accursed Share: Volume II & III*, p. 80

68   *Op. Cit.*, p. 132

69   Descartes, René (2003) *Meditations and Other Philosophical Writings*, p. 62

70   Nietzsche, Friedrich (1968) *The Will to Power*, p. 268 §484

71   Nishida, Kitarō (1987) *Last Writings*

72   Dōgen, quoted in Kitarō Nishida, *Op. Cit.*, p. 80

73   *Op. Cit.* p. 84

74   Lacan, Jacques (2008) "The Mirror Stage" in *Ecrits: a selection*

75   *Op. Cit.*, p. 6

76   Nishida, Kitarō (1987) *Last Writings*, p. 84

77   Nietzsche, Friedrich (2003) *The Birth of Tragedy*, p. 17

78   Camus, Albert (1975) *The Myth of Sisyphus*, p. 24

79   Kohn, Eduardo (2013) *How Forests Think*

80   Proust, Marcel (2000) *In Search of Lost Time Volume VI: Time Regained*, London: Vintage

81   Proust, Marcel (2000) *In Search of Lost Time Volume IV: Sodom and Gomorrah*, London: Vintage, p. 160: "When Albertine had gone, I remembered that I had promised Swann that I would write to Gilberte, and courtesy, I felt, demanded that I should do so at once. It was without emotion, and as though finishing off a boring school essay, that I traced upon the

envelope the name *Gilberte Swann* with which at one time I used to cover my exercise-books to give myself the illusion that I was corresponding with her. For if, in the past, it had been I who wrote that name, now the task had been deputed by Habit to one of the many secretaries whom she employs. He could write down Gilberte's name all the more calmly in that, placed with me only recently by Habit, having but recently entered my service, he had never known Gilberte, and knew only, without attaching any reality to the words, because he had heard me speak of her, that she was a girl with whom I had once been in love."

82   Deleuze, Gilles & Guattari, Felix (2004) *A Thousand Plateaus*, p. 249

83   Bataille, Georges (2012) *Eroticism*, p. 55

84   Garcia, Tristan (2014) *Form and Object*

85   Thacker, Eugene (2010) *After Life*

86   Huxley, Thomas Henry (1852) *Upon Animal Individuality*

87   Bergson, Henri (1998) *Creative Evolution*, p. 45

88   Haraway, Donna (1991) "Situated Knowledges: The Science Question in Feminism and the Privilege of Partial Perspective" in *Simians, Cyborgs and Women*, p. 183-201

89   Nishida, Kitarō (1987) *Last Writings*, p. 89

90   Spinoza (1910) *Short Treatise on God, Man and His Wellbeing*

91   Deleuze, Gilles & Guattari, Felix (2011) *Anti-Oedipus*, p. 105

92   Smith, Myron L, Bruhn, Johann N. & Anderson, James B. (1992) "The fungus Armillaria bulbosa is among the largest and oldest living organisms," in *Nature* vol. 356, p. 428-31

93   Brasier, Clive (1992) "A Champion Thallus," in *Nature,* vol. 356, p. 382-3

94   Badiou, Alain (2012) *Being and Event*

95   Bataille, Georges (2012) *Literature and Evil*

96   Deleuze, Gilles & Guattari, Felix (2004) *A Thousand Plateaus*, p. 239-40

97   Turner (2000) *The Extended Organism: The Physiology of Animal-Built Structures*, p. 19-24

98   Whitehead, Alfred North (2004) *The Concept of Nature*, p. 22

99   Guattari, Felix (2008) *The Three Ecologies*, p. 42-3

100 Turner, Scott J. (2000) *The Extended Organism*

101 Heraclitus (n.d.) *The Fragments*

102 Deleuze, Gilles & Guattari, Felix (2004) *A Thousand Plateaus*, p. 275

103 Heidegger, Martin (2000) *Introduction to Metaphysics*

104 Deleuze, Gilles (2004) *Difference and Repetition*, p. 96

105 Bataille, Georges (2008) *On Nietzsche*

106 Proust, Marcel (2000) *In Search of Lost Time Volume XI: Time Regained*

107 Borges, Jorge Luis (1998) "Funes, His Memory" in *Fictions*, p. 99

108 Kohn, Eduardo (2013) *How Forests Think*

109 Borges, *Op. Cit.*, pp. 99

110 Klossowski, Pierre (2008) *Nietzsche and the Vicious Circle*, p. 25

111 *Op. Cit.*

112 Deleuze, Gilles (1984) *Kant's Critical Philosophy*, p. xii

113 Bataille, Georges (2012) *Literature and Evil*

114 *Op. Cit.*

115 Derrida, Jacques (1998) *Of Grammatology*, p. 158

116 Latour, Bruno (2007) *Reassembling the Social*, p. 255

117 Tarde, Gabriel (2012) *Monadology and Sociology*

118 Kohn, Eduardo (2013) *How Forests Think*

119 Deleuze, Gilles & Guattari, Felix (2004) *A Thousand Plateaus*

120 Lienhardt, Godfrey (1978) *Divinity and Experience*, pp. 34-5

121 *Op Cit.*, p. 34

122 Bataille, Georges (2007a) *The Accursed Share: Volume I*, p. 213

123 *Op. Cit.*, p. 218

124 Aeschylus (1968) *Prometheus Bound, The Suppliants, Seven Against Thebes, The Persians*, p. 35

125 Novalis (1997) *Philosophical Writings*, p. 115; see also Stiegler, Bernard (2013) *What Makes Life Worth Living*

126 Heidegger, Martin (1977) "The Question Concerning Technology" in *The Question Concerning Technology and Other Essays*

127 Stiegler, Bernard (1998) *Technics and Time: The Fault of Epimetheus*, p. 17

128 Bergson, Henri (1998) *Creative Evolution*, New York: Dover

129 *Op. Cit.*, p. 107

130 Leroi-Gourhan, André (1993) *Gesture and Speech*

131 Wark, McKenzie (2014) *The Birth of Thanaticism*

132 Marx, Karl (1993) *Grundrisse*

133 Marx, Karl (1986) *Capital: Volume One*, p. 493-4 f3; see also Stiegler, Bernard (1998) *Technics and Time*, p. 26

134 Marx, *Op. Cit.*

135 Stiegler, Bernard (1998) *Technics and Time*, p. 49

136 Deleuze, Gilles & Guattari, Felix (2004) *A Thousand Plateaus*, p. 479

137 Heidegger, Martin (1977) *The Question Concerning Technology and Other Essays*, p. 35

138 Turner, J. Scott (2000) *The Extended Organism*

139 *Op. Cit.*

140 Lefebvre, Henri (1991) *The Production of Space*, p. 101

141 Hundertwasser, Friedensreich (1964) *Mouldiness Manifesto*

142 Heidegger, Martin (n.d.) *Building Dwelling Thinking*

143 Aeschylus (1968) *Prometheus Bound, The Suppliants, Seven Against Thebes, The Persians*, p. 35

144 Deleuze, Gilles & Guattari, Felix (2011) *Anti-Oedipus*, p. 96

145 Deleuze, Gilles (1988) *Spinoza: Practical Philosophy*, p. 19

146 Freud, Sigmund (1997) *The Interpretation of Dreams*

147 Kohn, Eduardo (2013) *How Forests Think*

148 Stanner, WEH (1979) "The Dreaming (1953)" in *White Man Got No Dreaming*, p. 29

149   *Op. Cit.*, p. 27

150   *Op. Cit.*, p. 28

151   Ingold, Tim (2007) *Lines: A Brief History*; and Ingold, Tim (2015) *The Life of Lines*

152   Heidegger, Martin (1977) "The Question Concerning Technology" in *The Question Concerning Technology and Other Essays*, p. 35

153   Myers, Fred R (1991) *Pintupi Country, Pintupi Self*

154   Stanner, WEH (1979) "The Dreaming (1953)" in *White Man Got No Dreaming*, p. 36

155   Haraway, Donna (2008) *When Species Meet*

156   Stanner, *Op. Cit.*, p. 36

157   Freud, Sigmund (2005) *On Murder, Mourning and Melancholia*, p. 205

158   Viveiros de Castro, Eduardo (1992) *From The Enemy's Point of View*, p. 196

159   Derrida, Jacques (2001) *The Work of Mourning*, p. 55

160   *Op. Cit.*, p. 143

161   Derrida, Jacques (1994) *Spectres of Marx*, p. xvii

162   Heidegger, Martin (1977) *The Question Concerning Technology and Other Essays*, pp. 8-9

163   McKenzie, Wark (2015) *Molecular Red*

164   Heidegger, *Op. Cit.*, p. 7

165   *Op. Cit.*

166   Klossowski, Pierre (2009) *Nietzsche and the Vicious Circle*, p. xvii

167   Marx, Karl (1844) *Economic and Philosophical Manuscripts*

168   *Op Cit.*

169   *Op Cit.*

170   *Op Cit.*

171   Marx, Karl (1843) *Contribution to the Critique of Hegel's Philosophy of Right*

172   Marx, Karl (1844) *Economic and Philosophical Manuscripts*

173 Bataille, Georges (2012) *Eroticism*, p. 44

174 *Op. Cit.*, p. 45

175 *Op. Cit.*, p. 47

176 Viveiros de Castro, Eduardo (1992) *From the Enemy's Point of View*, p. 196

177 Stiegler, Bernard (2013), *For a New Critique of Political Economy*

178 Marx, Karl (1986) *Capital: Volume 1*, pp. 873-940

179 Federici, Silvia (2009) *Caliban and the Witch*

180 Stiegler, Bernard (2013) *For a New Critique of Political Economy*, p. 33

181 Marx, Karl (1844) *Economic and Philosophical Manuscripts* in Fromm, Eric (2004) *Marx's Concept of Man*, p. 89

182 Bataille, Georges (2007a) *The Accursed Share: Volume I*, p. 134

183 Stiegler, Bernard (2013) *For a New Critique of Political Economy*, p. 38

184 Berardi, Franco Bifo (2009) *The Soul at Work*, p. 188

185 *Op. Cit.*

186 Viveiros de Castro, Eduardo (1992) *From The Enemy's Point of View*, p. 196

187 Derrida, Jacques (1994) *Given Time: I. Counterfeit Money*, p. 3

188 *Op. Cit*, p. 23

189 *Op. Cit.* p. 17

190 Borges, Jorge Luis (2000) "Funes, his Memory" in *Fictions*

191 Munn, Nancy (1992) *The Fame of Gawa*

192 Serres, Michel (2007) *The Parasite*

193 Derrida, Jacques (1994) *Given Time: I. Counterfeit Money*, p. 7

194 Bataille, Georges (2012) *Eroticism*, p. 42

195 Bergson, Henri (1998) *Creative Evolution*, p.

196 Deleuze, Gilles & Guattari, Felix (2004) *A Thousand Plateaus*, p. 479

197 Deleuze, Gilles (2004) *Difference and Repetition*, p. 96

198 DeLanda, Manuel (1997) *The Machinic Phylum*

199 Weiqiang, Li, Beard, Brian L. & Johnson, Clark M. (2015) *Biologically Recycled Continental Iron is a Major Component in Banded Iron Formations*

200 Novalis (1997) *Philosophical Writings*, p. 154

201 *Op. Cit.* p. 107

202 Bataille, Georges (2012) *Eroticism*, p. 42

203 *Op. Cit.*, p. 241

204 Baudrillard, Jean (2011) *Symbolic Exchange and Death*, p. 126

205 *Op. Cit.*, p.39

206 Fisher, Mark (2009) *Capitalist Realism*

207 Campagna, Federico (2013) *The Last Night*, p. 45

208 See Stiegler, Bernard (2013) *For A New Critique of Political Economy*; and Lazzarato, Maurizio (1996) "Immaterial Labour" in *Radical Thought in Italy*

209 Stiegler, Bernard (1998) *Technics and Time*, p. 6

Repeater Books

is dedicated to the creation of a new reality. The landscape of twenty-first-century arts and letters is faded and inert, riven by fashionable cynicism, egotistical self-reference and a nostalgia for the recent past. Repeater intends to add its voice to those movements that wish to enter history and assert control over its currents, gathering together scattered and isolated voices with those who have already called for an escape from Capitalist Realism. Our desire is to publish in every sphere and genre, combining vigorous dissent and a pragmatic willingness to succeed where messianic abstraction and quiescent co-option have stalled: abstention is not an option: we are alive and we don't agree.